Digital Culture & Society

Vol. 2, Issue 2/2016

Mark Coté, Paolo Gerbaudo, Jennifer Pybus (eds.)
Politics of Big Data

The journal is edited by
Pablo Abend, Mathias Fuchs, Ramón Reichert,
Annika Richterich, Karin Wenz

Editorial Board
Maria Bakardjieva, Brian Beaton, David Berry, Jean Burgess, Mark Coté, Colin Cremin, Sean Cubitt, Mark Deuze, José van Dijck, Delia Dumitrica, Astrid Ensslin, Sonia Fizek, Federica Frabetti, Richard A. Grusin, Orit Halpern, Irina Kaldrack, Wendy Hui Kyong Chun, Denisa Kera, Lev Manovich, Janet H. Murray, Jussi Parikka, Lisa Parks, Christiane Paul, Dominic Pettman, Rita Raley, Richard Rogers, Julian Rohrhuber, Marie-Laure Ryan, Mirko Tobias Schäfer, Jens Schröter, Trebor Scholz, Tamar Sharon, Roberto Simanowski, Nathaniel Tkacz, Nanna Verhoeff, Geoffrey Winthrop-Young, Sally Wyatt

[transcript]

The Journal *Digital Culture & Society* appears twice a year, in March (spring) and September (fall).
It is available for annual subscription directly from the publisher. The subscription begins with the current issue and includes all issues of one year. Delivery of the subscribed issues occurs immediately after their appearance. Invoicing occurs with delivery of the first issue of a year. The subscription is automatically continued by one year, unless canceled with the publisher by February 1st.

For more information, please see: http://transcript-verlag.de/dcs

Bibliographic information published by the Deutsche Nationalbibliothek
The Deutsche Nationalbibliothek lists this publication in the Deutsche Nationalbibliografie; detailed bibliographic data are available on the Internet at http://dnb.d-nb.de

© 2016 transcript Verlag, Bielefeld

All rights reserved. No part of this book may be reprinted or reproduced or utilized in any form or by any electronic, mechanical, or other means, now known or hereafter invented, including photocopying and recording, or in any information storage or retrieval system, without permission in writing from the publisher.

Cover layout: Kordula Röckenhaus, Bielefeld
Typeset: Michael Rauscher, Bielefeld

ISSN 2364-2114
eISSN 2364-2122
Print-ISBN 978-3-8376-3211-8
PDF-ISBN 978-3-8394-3211-2

Content

Introduction
Politics of Big Data
Mark Coté, Paolo Gerbaudo and Jennifer Pybus   5

Critiquing Big Data

What Counts?
Reflections on the Multivalence of Social Media Data
Carolin Gerlitz   19

Big Data and the Paradox of Diversity
Bernhard Rieder   39

Digital Epistemologies

The Alternative Epistemologies of Data Activism
Stefania Milan, Lonneke van der Velden   57

Simondon on Datafication
A Techno-Cultural Method
Mark Coté, Jennifer Pybus   75

Digital Methodologies

From Data Analytics to Data Hermeneutics
Online Political Discussions, Digital Methods and
the Continuing Relevance of Interpretive Approaches
Paolo Gerbaudo   95

Visual Social Media and Big Data
Interpreting Instagram Images Posted on Twitter
Dhiraj Murthy, Alexander Gross, Marisa McGarry   113

Entering the Field

Group Privacy in Times of Big Data
A Literature Review
Paula Helm   137

Biographical Notes   153

Introduction
Politics of Big Data

Mark Coté, Paolo Gerbaudo and Jennifer Pybus

This special issue offers a critical dialogue around the myriad political dimensions of Big Data. We begin by recognising that the technological objects of Big Data are unprecedented in the speed, scope and scale of their computation and knowledge production. This critical dialogue is grounded in an equal recognition of continuities around Big Data's social, cultural, and political economic dimensions. Big Data, then, is political in the same way in which identity, the body, gender, sexuality, race and ethnicity are political, that is, as sites of struggle over meaning, interpretations, and categorisations of lived experience. Big Data is political in the way circuits of production, distribution, and consumption are political; that is, as sites where access, control and agency are unequally distributed through asymmetrical power relations, including relations of data production. Big Data is political in the way contemporary politics are being reshaped by data analysis in electoral campaign strategy, and through state surveillance as strikingly evidenced by the Snowden revelations on the NSA and GCHQ. Big Data is also political in the contestation of this advanced scientific practice, wherein the generation of data at unprecedented scale promises a precise and objective measure of everyday life. However, the computational dreams of an N = all verisimilitude – that is, of datasets providing a one-to-one correspondence to a given phenomenon – are haunted by the normative biases embedded in all data. This is not to suggest that Big Data – more specifically processes of datafication[1] – are best or at all understood as socially constructed. Indeed, discursive analysis or unreconstructed social theory cannot fully grasp how data re-articulates the social, cultural, political and economic in a deeply recursive manner. Thus, any political reckoning must equally account for the materiality of data, alongside the logic guiding its processes and the practices that deploy its tools. In short, what are the power relations animating the knowledge generated by data analytics?

---

1   See Pybus et al. 2015; van Dijck 2014; Cukier/Mayer-Schonberger 2013 for detailed discussion of datafication.

No politics, just data?

As smartphones proliferated last decade, powerful computational media were diffused across time and space into a distributed networks of pervasive data generation. An apolitical vision of Big Data quickly followed. Prominent researchers seized on the potential of this data to fuel new forms of computational social science or what some termed 'social engineering' (Lazier et al. 2009). Enthusiasm for developing rigorous mathematical models and applications to understand and predict complex social phenomena reached a high point with Alex Pentland (2014). His MIT research lab developed a highly anodyne vision of "reality mining" (Eagle/Pentland 2006) our data-driven society, wherein the sheer deluge of data points would help attenuate previous limitations imposed by partial or incomplete samples. Reality mining, as proposed by Pentland, looks for social patterns in the quotidian data we generate to infer our relationships, significant locations and actions. This is done to model individual behaviour and organisational rhythms with the goal of predicting future phenomena. Broadly, data scientists tend to follow such practices, when data mining, to derive meaning from social and cultural analytics.

The trope of the enormity of Big Data is now well established, with constantly updating numbers: 95% of all data was created in the past two years; data doubles in size every two years; the number of smartphones will soon nearly equal the world's population; within five years there will be an estimated 50 billion smart connected devices; and currently less than 1% of all data is ever analysed or used (Marr 2015). Datafication is one way of describing these technological processes that seek to transform life into data and then to reconstitute that data into actionable sites of value and insight. Kenneth Cukier and Viktor Mayer-Schoenberger (2013) initiated the concept of datafication as a neutral descriptor for data as a resource, harvested from our words, actions, connections, locations, bodies, infrastructures and natural environments in which we live. Datafication is thus presented as an innovative value generator, primarily through business intelligence or market insight about what we think, how we feel, what we respond to, where we go, what we do, who we interact with, what we listen to, what we read, what we like, who we like, and so on. Such pervasive reach drives neutral and anodyne visions of datafication: faith that with enough data comes truth. So "if we collect all the data – 'n = all,' to use the terminology of statistics – the problem [of samples or of data modelling] disappears" (Cukier/Mayer-Schoenberger 2013: p. 30). Big Data is thereby driven by a resolution of verisimilitude: not just faith but an actual resolve that if we just gather enough data, its finely granulated resolution will reveal in high definition all the world's hidden truths.

Some go as far as to suggest that the Big Data age means we no longer need models for understanding. Chris Anderson was an early advocate of this new Big Data vision, and at the core of his 'end of theory' thesis was a simple idea: "Petabytes allow us to say: 'Correlation is enough'" (2008). This new-found power of correlation is stoked by an equal belief that if individual human behaviour can be mined at an adequate depth, then there is little need for a more structural understandings of businesses, organisations, markets and indeed, virtually every other social, cultural, political and natural phenomena. Pentland even suggests that Big Data renders scholars such as Adam Smith or Karl Marx to the data-poor dustbin of history: "[markets and classes] are aggregates. They're averages. While it may be useful to reason about the averages, social phenomena are really made up of millions of small transactions between individuals" (Pentland 2012).

Data Power and Knowledge

This 'no politics, just data' paradigm has garnered sustained and widespread critique. A cursory overview might include danah boyd and Kate Crawford's (2011) early questioning of the underlying drive of Big Data; namely the pursuit of maximising value from as much data as possible by both industry and the State. So immediately, a politics of Big Data faces the question of value for whom? For advertisers? For policing? For state security? For new pricing models or service delivery? And how does this question of value relate to communities, especially outside of market relations? Other critiques, such as the the one put forward by Lisa Gitelman (2013) have attacked the very premise of 'raw' data, outlining the myriad ways in which all data are 'cooked' or constructed, thereby demystifying claims of clean, unfiltered and neutral data. Similarly, Rasmus Helles and Klaus Bruhn Jensen (2013) remind us that data making is a complex process that involves multiple agents. Farida Vis (2013) critically reflects on how both researchers and the tools they use fundamentally impact on both data access and quality. Meanwhile, for questions of interpretation, value and meaning scale up with large data sets, which poses complex methodological challenges (Busch 2014). These get articulated both in terms of the data itself – from its provenance to its political economy – to the interpretive techniques deployed to generate meaning or actionability. José van Dijck (2014) contends that this rampant growth of large social datasets is fueled by a widespread public willingness to share personal information on corporate platforms; she calls this 'dataism', a secular belief in precisely those anodyne qualities of data. Dataism is the public counterpart to the scientific and professional paradigm previously outlined, bringing us to a danger inherent in an unreflective pursuit of ubiquitous data capture: dataveillance.

Many have used a Foucauldian frame to demonstrate the role of computers aiding surveillance (Lyon 1994). Greg Elmer (2003) highlighted the panoptic reach of the digital via Michel Foucault's 'diagrammatic approach'. This is resonant with our special issue, as it emphasises how digital panopticism engenders not just repressive but productive power relations. More recently, Tania Bucher (2012) notes how such panopticism encourages Facebook participation. Now under Big Data, the all-seeing gaze of social networks enacts a new threat: that one *might not* be seen and thereby rendered invisible in the data flows. This data imperative to be seen is as keenly pursued by the NSA or GCHQ as it is by industry and marketing practices: that is, the use of pervasive personal data systems to systematically monitor people and groups in order to regulate, govern, monitor and influence their behaviour (Degli Esposti 2014). Likewise, the Foucauldian dispositif has been used to examine the 'productive' counterpart of pervasive digital networked relations, as well as the materiality of power (Röhle 2005; Coté and Pybus 2007; Ruppert, Law and Savage 2013).

Alongside these fundamental critiques, the algorithm has become an important cipher for decrypting the various political dimensions of Big Data across society. Beer (2009), for example, theorises the algorithm as a form of data power, expressed in the now constitutive role of Big Data in popular culture and social life. A brief list on how algorithms enact new procedures of power and knowledge includes the biases of dataveillance as deployed in war scenarios and security apparatuses (Amoore 2009), in biometrics (Cheney-Lippold 2011), finance (Lenglet 2011), gaming (Galloway 2006), and how it can construct silos or 'filter bubbles' in political discourse, segmenting social life and the public sphere (Pariser 2011). Finally, Frank Pasquale (2015) notes how pervasive data gathering takes on a problematic political economic form when algorithmic black boxes are deployed in a proprietary and mostly unregulated market. Data, then, is always curated and defined, each time embedding values and biases into the algorithms – the step-by-step instructions – through which it will be processed. The insights, or actionable information will always be a product of those material processes. Or, as bluntly stated by Cathy O'Neill (2016), "We're pretending we are not embedding our values in algorithms and calling them neutral. That's bullshit."

A closely related dimension of data politics is political economic domination and control. Concentration of ownership and unprecedented market value are remarkable expressions of data power. Google is the world's most valuable company whose market value exceeds half a trillion dollars (in a near dead heat with Apple) while Facebook is the world's most popular digital platform, with 1.13 Billion daily active users. Such market power grows unabated in the hands of a few corporations across platforms and data infrastructures (McChesney 2013). Similarly, Vincent Mosco (2014) draws our attention to political economy of cloud computing by examining the ownership structures that governs the productions, processing, storage and distribution of the data that are stored in these vast and expansive closed systems. Such concentration of ownership of data opens questions about alternative ways of managing it, ranging from the creation of data commons accessible to researchers and communities (Pybus et al. 2016), to platform co-operatives (Scholz, 2016). At issue here is the general redistribution of value from data collection and analysis.

Concentrated market power, structural inequalities between data generation and control, alongside the rise of pervasive dataveillance and opaque algorithms that are executing predictive analytics with discriminatory results takes us some distance from an ameliorating realm of neutral Big Data. This special issue proposes no singular paradigm or conceptual frame for addressing the myriad elements and effects of the contemporary condition of the data human. It does, however, suggest that a political critique entails questions of data access, technological understanding and capacities, and the ability to critically examine the algorithms of data analytics in order to forensically unpack the value-laden information and knowledge produced. We suggest that one way of making the political dimensions of Big Data visible is from a broad Foucauldian perspective, as briefly indicated above. First, this can address the materiality of data by targeting the technical and architectural dimensions of power. These insights of the post-epistemic Foucault not only exceed the symbolic or discursive but also look to the inherently productive dimensions of power. Also, this situates Big Data – or even more specifically datafication – as a matrix for power-knowledge relations. This is crucial to the 'actionability' of Big Data which is expressed in a complex network of relations: combinatory processes that allow us to "see and speak".

There is a critical promise in broadly framing Big Data within power-knowledge relations. We have seen how datafication has made data a resource, and subjected everyday life to pressures of productivity, including instruments of control and biased or discriminatory categorisation. A general diagnostic approach helps unpack the ways in which data-power/knowledge both productively enables us to speak and be seen but also repressively catogorises, correlates and classifies us. A Foucauldian diagnostic of data knowledge frames it as "a form of knowledge that defines and determines differences ... [which] can permit a new objective field to appear" (Foucault 1996: 95). The notion of the objective field echoes the 'no politics just data' frame. Foucault, however, uses it to indicate how specific knowledge becomes visible in a given historical moment. Once, for Foucault, this was the sexual deviant, now, for Big Data, it is the bad credit subject derived from social network analysis. Both are instances of what Foucault called "articulated historical content" (96) facilitating knowledge production, 'objective' fields which categorise, ordering, and classify, expressing deeply asymmetrical relations of data access and agency. This can be taken up as a kind of data hermeneutic, one that entails an empirical – or material – examination of the conditions enabling if not truth claims, then actionability. Finally, there is one last Foucauldian inflection that helps emphasise the political stakes at play in Big Data. One model for the productive dimension of power was that of biopower, albeit expressed primarily in terms of control and domination (Foucault 1994). There is, however, the counterpoint of the biopolitical, as outlined by Lazzarato (2002) which emphasises the creativity and capacity for resistance inherent in power. We urge a similar understanding of Big Data: as a contested realm of *data power* and the *data political*.

Themes and Contributions on Politics and Big Data

The following contributions unfold across related themes exploring the data-politics nexus. First, Carolin Gerlitz and Bernhard Rieder unpack the power-knowledge relations of Big Data as they play out across social media platforms. Second, Big Data is explored not only as a means of political domination but as a critical and creative resource that can be utilised in a different direction by civil society groups and ordinary citizens. The contributions by Stefania Milan and Lonneke van der Velden and Mark Coté and Jennifer Pybus explore a range of approaches both for struggles over and for the democratization of Big Data. Third, are questions regarding the consequences inherent in the particular gaze afforded by Big Data and its classificatory techniques. Paolo Gerbaudo and Dhiraj Murthy, Alexander Gross and Marisa McGarry respectively explore concrete, political, social and organizational practices in relation to how to interpret and understand the content that gets uploaded on social media to empower the citizens that use such platforms. These articles show how Big Data is not just changing politics but also the way we can conduct research about political phenomena.

In the first paper, 'Big Data and the Paradox of Diversity', Bernhard Rieder takes us through a provocative argument that focuses less on the errors that arise from Big Data's empirical truth claims and more on the impact of data mining practices within contemporary capitalist societies. By so doing, he develops a critique built around the myriad ways in which data analysis is increasingly geared towards producing "actionable forms of knowledge" instead of "disinterested description." Rieder brings our attention to the ways in which empirical methods, such as what he calls 'accounting realism' are used for profitable decision making. For example, in looking at how spam filters operate, he describes how both decision models and machine learning algorithms help to ensure that these email filters are rendered more effective, based on their capacity to adapt and become personalised. What is of interest here lies in "the profound consequences for how decisions come to be made and how judgement is operationalized." Thus, it does not matter if the spam filter is always correct, rather that it works most of the time and can thereby be considered as a reliable tool to make a judgment. Similarly, as his argument progresses, this value based accounting realism slides into other areas of society wherein algorithms are being used.

The political objective of Rieder's intervention is precisely to add to our understanding of the "profound ideological role at the intersection of sociality, research, and commerce" (van Dijck 2014: 201). By considering how large quantities of data are amassed and analysed, he unpacks how these algorithmic practices have extended our unquestioned acceptance of productivity, performance, and merit or in his words 'economic morality' (Allen 2012). This more holistic perspective of Big Data leads him to consider the possibility of what it means if algorithms actually 'work.' Rieder therefore urges us to think through the limitations and biases of Big Data but equally to consider how this growing capacity to know society via performative forms of judgment may become a "mode of governing through measuring."

In the second paper, "What Counts? Reflections on the Multivalence of Social Media Data," Carolin Gerlitz critically examines how value is inscribed in the social data that is generated on platforms. Drawing on both platform and valuation studies, she argues that the social media are multivalent sites of production, and thus a platform must cater to a range of different actors including users, advertisers, media outlets, or other corporate partners. The paper explores the specific socio-technical conditions wherein processes of valuation are always already inscribed into the programmability and affordances, alongside the constraints that govern the sociality of a platform's stakeholders. Within this framework, where the production of value becomes plural, Gerlitz argues that platform (pre)formed data is governed by different 'grammars of action'. In short, "valuable alongside multiple, conflicting value regimes." The sites of capture, which are then built into the networked circuits of sociality, should not be understood as singular sites of economic valorization. Instead, the different processes of valuation will ensure that the social data that gets generated will contribute to the enactment of multiple, albeit conflicting, value registers within the platform. And so, drawing on Badiou she asks: "What counts in the sense of what is valued? – is that which is counted. Conversely, everything that can be numbered must be valued."

Drawing on Instagram as a case study, Gerlitz argues for a critical account on platforms. Within the brief methodological experiment that she outlines, based on a workshop that was conducted during the Digital Methods Winter School at the University of Amsterdam, she demonstrates the competing tensions that exist between different grammars of action (both front and back end). The frictions that arises can be seen in relation to a number of decisions made by Instagram in late 2015. The changes, however, that were brought about by the social media platform were aimed at recalibrating user engagement and worked to maximize their exposure to paid content or advertising. Gerlitz concludes by asking us to consider the plurality of ways in which the conditions of valuation are inscribed to devise alternative accounts of 'what counts'.

In the third paper, Stefania Milan and Lonneke van der Velden discuss different forms of activism which make data a new terrain of contention. The authors highlight how different campaigns and social movements approach the question of Big Data. For some, Big Data is mainly understood in terms of a threat to individual rights, and to privacy. For others, Big Data has more positive possibilities, allowing new opportunities for social change. A number of examples of data activism are covered, from the social media forensics of Elliot Higgins, to Open Source Intelligence, and the Occupy Data group a spinoff of Occupy Wall Street. Data activism is defined as a "series of sociotechnical practices that, emerging at the fringes of the contemporary activism ecology, critically interrogate datafication and its socio-political consequences". This type of activism is in continuity with previous forms of activism that has also involved demonstrating the political potential of information, among them statactivsim: a port-manteau of statistics and activism. However, Milan and van der Velden introduce a new element, reflecting the techniques and forms of knowledge associated with data production and distribution. The article goes on to examine the productive and creative character of data activism, and relates this to the new ways in which using data are developed. Moreover, it provides a mapping of different forms of data activism, along the axis reactive-proactive and individual-collective. In so doing, the authors demonstrate how data activism has by now become a diversified area of political activism and campaigning – one that is likely to see great developments in years to come.

In the fourth paper, Mark Coté and Jennifer Pybus extend their research on new forms of critical and creative data agency (Pybus et al. 2016) through a focus on interdisciplinary workshop which bring together humanities researchers and social scientists with coders and hackers. They suggest the hacker ethos and practice of critical engagement with technology has pedagogical value to strategically counter the tendency toward control and value extraction, which currently dominates processes of datafication. Coté and Pybus report upon their workshop 'Hacking the Mobile Ecosystem' which opened up mobile applications to their constituent elements, in this case exposing and exploring the coding of permissions which calibrate the harvesting and flows of our personal data. The authors evince political efficacy in theorising such interdisciplinary practices as a 'techno-cultural' method via the work of the French philosopher of technology Gilbert Simondon. This is practice-led theory, where the workshop acts as a zone of interdisciplinary translation, not just for otherwise hidden technical elements facilitating data flows, but as a means to articulate socio-cultural and political-economic dimensions.

The authors argue for the workshop to be understood as more than a site for the development of technical skills in the use of digital tools for either computational methods in humanities or empirical research. Instead, Coté and Pybus assert a basic political orientation for the techno-cultural method: to critically unpack the data materiality of the human condition under datafication. The workshop is thus seen as a practical articulation of Simondon's notion of 'difficult humanism' which integrates human and technical reality, that is technology into culture. The authors put forward Simondon's technicity as the conceptual key of the techno-cultural method. Technicity coheres the elements of any technical object yet it is also an excess which always exceeds the its apparent instrumentality. Coté and Pybus thus present a two-fold political elaboration through the opening up of technical objects. First, it makes visible constituted power and control, engaging the normative and regulatory dimensions of technical objects which inscribe us more deeply into circuits of production and consumption. But crucially, techno-cultural workshops also seek the super abundance of technicity in the technical object, practically engaging those elements as the potential energy to differently organise collective life beyond normative systems.

In the fifth paper, Dhiraj Murthy, Alexander Gross and Marisa McGarry focus on event-based datafication, specifically how it impacts the changing ways in which natural disasters are experienced, as well as how they can be studied. Where once journalists might have been considered as the gatekeepers of content, the volume of social media commentary and images have had a profound impact on the ways in which such collective moments are both represented and experienced by the public. By focusing on Hurricane Sandy, which occurred on October 29th, 2012, the authors draw on Big Data methodologies to highlight how critical empirical-based work can be used to better understand those latent narratives which may exist within visual social media data. They therefore developed a case study of 11,964 geolocated images that were taken by users on Instagram and then embedded on Twitter.

Murthy, Gross and McGarry were drawn to this natural disaster, given it was the first of its kind wherein not only did Instagram play a significant role in shaping public discourse and understanding of Hurricane Sandy but was also the first and last major US event in which Twitter and Instagram came together. In short, creating unique circumstances, wherein images were networked across two platforms by citizens who were collectively experiencing the hurricane as it unfolded. As a result, the authors' findings demonstrate that the number of selfies posted or pictures with food and drink, pets among other humorous images highlighted the possibility of the change in the politics of representation as it relates to natural disasters. Here social media users are seen as informed subjects, signalling the informal and ironic way in which citizens rather than authorities conceive of and communicate disaster situations. Thus, the article shows that it is necessary to explore further the actual content of social media conversations, and that from this analysis it is possible to understand the specific angle and attitude that is dominant in a conversation, as well as the politics that are at play within it.

The article by Paolo Gerbaudo proposes the notion of data hermeneutics as an alternative and qualitative supplement to data analytics for the study of social media data. Gerbaudo argues that data analytics has become something akin to an orthodoxy in the field of digital politics and social media research, leading to a quantitative bias that is accompanied by a neglect for the actual content and meaning of online conversations. To move beyond this situation, Gerbaudo proposes that it is necessary to recuperate some key insights from the hermeneutic tradition as it has developed in a number of field from phenomenology, to literary criticism, qualitative sociology and anthropology. In particular, it is urgent to reassert the hermeneutic preoccupation with interpretation and the understanding that phenomena must be excavated at greater depth by looking at the deep structure of meaning and connected discourses. However, this task entails a digital update of hermeneutic procedures, traditionally concerned with textual study (poems, novels, films ec.), but now inclusive of the study of social media data. Referring to Paul Ricœur, Gerbaudo argues that data hermeneutics needs to "approach data as the 'inscription' or recorded trace of a peculiar form of social text: social media conversations". This is a radically different view of social media data, from the one of data analytics that sees social media posts as transparent and discrete data-points. Furthermore, data hermeneutics needs to revise the close reading approach of literary criticism, making the object of close reading specific social media posts, and the larger conversations in which they are immersed. The article thus sketches out a research strategy and ethos which asserts the value of data hermeneutics as a necessary counterpart to data analytics.

(Finally, the publishing of this special issue was supervised by Ramón Reichert.)

References

Allen, Ansgar (2012): "Life Without the 'X' Factor: Meritocracy Past and Present." In: Power and Education 4/1, pp. 4–19.
Amoore, Louise (2009): "Algorithmic war: Everyday geographies of the war on terror." In: Antipode 41/1, pp. 49–69.
Anderson, Chris (2008): "The end of theory." In: Wired, 16/June 23 (http://archive.wired.com/science/discoveries/magazine/16-07/pb_theory).
Beer, David (2009): "Power through the algorithm? Participatory web cultures and the technological Unconscious." In: New Media & Society 11/6, pp. 985–1002.
boyd, danah/Crawford, Kate (2011): "Six provocations for Big Data." In: Social Science Research Network (http://papers.ssrn.com/sol3/papers.cfm?abstract_id=1926431).
Busch, Lawrence (2014): "A Dozen Ways to Get Lost in Translation: Inherent Challenges in Large-Scale Data Sets." In: International Journal of Communication 8, pp. 1727–1744.
Bucher, Tania (2012): "Want to be on the top? Algorithmic power and the threat of invisibility on Facebook." In: New Media & Society 14/7, pp. 1164–1180.
Cheney-Lippold, John (2011): "A new algorithmic identity: Soft biopolitics and the modulation of control." In: Theory, Culture & Society 28/6, pp. 164–181.
Coté, Mark/Pybus, Jennifer (2007): "Learning to Immaterial Labour 2.0: MySpace and Social Networks." In: Ephemera 7/1: pp. 88–106.
Cukier, Kenneth/Mayer-Schonberger, Viktor (2013): Big Data: A Revolution That Will Transform How We Live, Work and Think, London: John Murray.
Degli Esposti, Sara (2014): "When Big Data meets dataveillance: The hidden side of analytics." In: Surveillance & Society 12/2, pp. 209–225.
Eagle, Nathan/Pentland, Alex (2006): "Reality mining: Sensing complex social systems." In: Personal Ubiquitous Computing 10, pp. 255–268.
Elmer, Greg (2003): "A Diagram of Panoptic Surveillance." In: New Media & Society 5/2, pp. 231–47.
Foucault, Michel (1994): "Les mailles du pouvoir." In: Daniel Defert/François Ewald (eds.), Dits et écrits: Tome IV, Éditions Gallimard, Paris, pp. 182–201.
Foucault, Michel (1996): Foucault Live, New York: Semiotext(e).
Galloway, Alex (2006): Gaming: Essays on Algorithmic Culture, Minneapolis: University of Minnesota Press.
Gitelman, Lisa (2013): "Raw Data" is an Oxymoron, Cambridge, MA: MIT Press.

Helles, Rasmus/Jensen, Klaus Bruhn (2013): "Making data – Big Data and beyond." In: First Monday 18/10 (http://firstmonday.org/article/view/4860/3748).

Jordan, Tim (2015): Information Politics: Liberation and Exploitation in the Digital Society, London: Pluto Press.

Lazzarato, Maurizio (2002): "From Biopower to Biopolitics." In: Pli: The Warwick Journal of Philosophy 13, pp. 112–125.

Lazer, David et al. (2009): "Life in the network: The coming age of computational social science." In: Science 323/5915, pp. 721–723.

Lenglet, Marc (2011): "Conflicting codes and Codings: How algorithmic trading is reshaping financial regulation." In: Theory, Culture & Society 28/6, pp. 44–66.

Lyon, David (1994): The Electronic Eye: The Rise of Surveillance Society, Minneapolis: University of Minnesota Press.

Marr, Bernard (2015): "Big Data: 20 Mind-Boggling Facts Everyone Must Read." In: Forbes, September 30 (http://www.forbes.com/sites/bernardmarr/2015/09/30/big-data-20-mind-boggling-facts-everyone-must-read/#22a3feff6c1d).

McChesney, Robert W. (2013): Digital disconnect: How capitalism is turning the Internet against democracy, New York: The New Press.

Mosco, Vincent (2014): To the Cloud: Big Data in a Turbulent World, New York: Routledge.

O'Neill, Cathy (2016): "Weapons of Math Destruction." Lecture at King's College London, September 28.

Pariser, Eli (2011): The Filter Bubble: What the Internet Is Hiding from You, New York: Viking.

Pasquale, Frank (2015): The Black Box Society: The Secret Algorithms That Control Money and Information, Cambridge, MA: Harvard University Press.

Pentland, Sandy (2012): "Reinventing Society in the Wake of Big Data." In: Edge, Oct. 20 (https://www.edge.org/conversation/alex_sandy_pentland-reinventing-society-in-the-wake-of-big-data).

Pentland, Sandy (2014): Social Physics: How Good Ideas Spread – The Lessons from a New Science, New York: Penguin Books.

Pybus, Jennifer/Coté, Mark/Blanke Tobias (2015): "Hacking the Social Life of Big Data." In: Big Data & Society 2/2, pp. 26–33.

Rohle, Theo (2005): "Power, reason, closure: Critical perspectives on new media theory." In: New Media and Society 7/3, pp. 403–422.

Ruppert, Evelyn/Law, John/Savage, Mike (2013): "Rethinking Empirical Social Sciences." In: Theory, Culture & Society 30/4, pp. 22–46.

Scholz, Trebor (2016): Platform Coorperativism. Challlenging the Corporate Sharing Economy, New York: Rosa Luxemburg Stiftung.

van Dijck, Jose (2014): "Datafication, dataism and dataveillance: Big Data between scientific paradigm and ideology." In: Surveillance & Society 12/2, pp. 197–208.

Vis, Farida (2013). "A Critical Reflection on Big Data: Considering APIs, researchers and tools as data makers." In: First Monday 18/10 (http://firstmonday.org/ojs/index.php/fm/article/view/4878).

Critiquing Big Data

What Counts?
Reflections on the Multivalence of Social Media Data

Carolin Gerlitz

Abstract

Social media platforms have been characterised by their programmability, affordances, constraints and stakeholders – the question of value and valuation of platforms, their data and features has, however, received less attention in platform studies. This paper explores the specific socio-technical conditions for valuating platform data and suggests that platforms set up their data to become multivalent, that is to be valuable alongside multiple, possibly conflicting value regimes. Drawing on both platform and valuation studies, it asks how the production, storing and circulation of data, its connection to user action and the various stakeholders of platforms contribute to its valuation. Platform data, the paper suggests, is the outcome of capture systems which allow to collapse action and its capture into pre-structured data forms which remain open to divergent interpretations. Platforms offer such grammars of action both to users and other stakeholders in front- and back-ends, inviting them to produce and engage with its data following heterogeneous orders of worth. Platform data can participate in different valuation regimes at the same time – however, the paper concludes, not all actors can participate in all modes of valuation, as in the end, it is the platform that sets the conditions for participation. The paper offers a conceptual perspective to interrogate what data counts by attending to questions of quantification, its entanglement with valuation and the various technologies and stakeholders involved. It finishes with an empirical experiment to map the various ways in which Instagram data is made to count.

Keywords: Big data; digital methods; platform data; back-end; infrastructures of evaluation.

Introduction

From the very beginning of social media platforms, their data has been approached as a source of value – economic, social, cultural or political value. In economic contexts social media data is considered valuable as it allows to identify consumer preferences and relations (Turow 2006), can be made relevant for risk assessment (Amoore 2011), brand valuation (Moor & Lury 2011), behavioural targeting (Turow 2012), or the prediction of financial markets. In social contexts, platform data bears value as it is considered to account for attention, connectedness or reputation (Paßmann & Gerlitz 2014; Hearn 2010). In relation to the political sphere, social media not only provide insights into controversies or topical affairs (Marres & Moats 2015), but also into bias (Borra & Weber 2012), electoral preferences or intelligence concerns, thus potentially bearing political value. Social media platforms, media studies scholars argue, operate across these value registers, as they enable communication, whilst at the same time transforming it into economically valuable data, allowing for what Langlois and Elmer understand as "double articulation" (2013) of different value registers.

Whereas the issue of value has been central to debates about *social media data*, it has surfaced less prominently in the context of *platform studies* which explore the technical infrastructures involved in data production and processing. However, in order to discuss the valuation of data, one needs to account for the socio-technical conditions of its making. Platforms have been explored regarding their programmability or, as Bogost and Montfort put it, their capacities to be built upon (2009), their expansion into the web or into app spaces (Helmond 2015a), or into other platforms through cross-syndication and interoperability (Bodle 2011). Such techno-materialist perspectives in platform studies are currently being advanced by fostering the intersections between platform and infrastructure studies (Helmond 2015b; Plantin et al. 2016; see also Schuettpelz & Gießmann 2015), a strand that considers platforms as one of the infrastructure providers of communication. Other scholarship attends to the affordances and constraints for communication and sociality enabled by platforms, attending to the possibilities platforms offer to users through their front-end or to developers in the back-end (Bucher 2013; Gillespie 2010). This strand of platform studies outlines the limits and restrictions of platform features and draws attention to the ways in which platforms enable, but also channel, modulate and restrain expression (Crawford & Gillespie, 2014; Dijck, 2013a). A third strand outlines the involvement of the multiple and heterogeneous stakeholders (Gillespie 2010; Bodle 2011) to which platforms cater to. Platforms simultaneously try to address private users, who seek to communicate and socialise; companies, who want to market their business; analysts, who try to understand consumers; or politicians and organisation, who strive to engage – just to name a few. Many of these stakeholders are being approached through distinct interfaces – Instagram for instance has dedicated interfaces for users, developers, advertisers and businesses. To bring together the heterogeneous objectives of their stakeholders with their own business aims, platforms may need to unfold a series of politics (Gillespie 2010) and organise the conditions within which different actors can participate in their data and features. This short overview surely cannot give justice to the various strands in platform studies – rather it should outline that platforms have been conceptualised as creating the socio-technical conditions for various stakeholders to pursue their interests and are subject to constant enactment, forming a "set of relations that constantly needs to be performed,' in part due to continual friction between, on one side, users' goals of expression and, on the other side, platforms' profit-seeking aims and the legal surround that defines legitimate use" (van Dijck, 2013a: 26).

Whilst the technical conditions for bringing these stakeholders together have been explored from different perspectives, the question how platforms are informed by the valuation of their data is one that requires further attention. The objective of this paper is thus to add to existing platform scholarship a discussion on how social media data is made valuable and how these valuation processes are entangled with the platform's other characteristics, namely programmability, affordances/constraints and stakeholder involvement. It does so by drawing on a plural account of value. Social sciences have been informed by a bifurcation between *value* – referring to economic value or profit – and *values* – referring to the multiplicity of social norms (Graeber 2006). In this paper, however, I am mainly interested in different value registers social media data can speak to which operate beyond the value/values distinction and suggest to treat value in a plural way, including all forms of value, social, economic, political etc. Engaging with valuation studies (Vatin 2013) this paper further differentiates between evaluation – that is the process of value assessment – and valuation – the process of value production. Valuation is further preferred over valorisation, as the former addresses the production of different forms of value, whilst the latter is mainly used to refer to economic value creation (Vatin 2013). Such pluralist accounts of key terms are necessary to account for the multiplicity of value regimes at stake in platforms. The paper is driven by the following questions: What are the socio-technical conditions of valuation of platform data and alongside which value registers is social media data made valuable? It puts forwards the claim that social media platform data is created to be multi-valent (Marres 2009; Gerlitz 2012), that is to speak to more than one value register at the same time and sets out to expand the characteristics of social media platforms.

It does so by attending to different facets of the question "What counts?" and by creating an initial dialogue between platform studies and scholarship on valuation (Vatin 2013). In a first step, the paper discusses the relation between platforms and multivalence, drawing on previous contributions on the enactment of multiple value registers. Then it attends to the socio-technical condition for producing and recombining social media data, focusing especially on quantification and standardisation in form: "What counts in the sense of what is valued – is that which is counted. Conversely, everything that can be numbered must be valued" Alain Badiou suggests (2008: 1) and this nexus between countability and valorisation is attended to by conceptualising platform affordances and constraints as "grammars of action" (Agre 1994). Platform data, the paper claims, is produced to be standardised in form and flexible in meaning – and thus valuation. The paper draws on examples from Facebook, Twitter and Instagram. The latter is especially focused on and drawing on an empirical experiment the paper asks how different actors realise the value of platform data differently by mapping apps build on top of the platform. The conclusion reflects on the limits of distributed valuation in the case of social media platform data by asking who can participate in the process of valorisation and valuation and on what grounds?

On platforms and multiple value registers

The term platform, Gillespie notes (2010), emerged as a self-description of social media corporations who sought to fashion themselves as neutral content intermediaries (see also Helmond 2015 on the term platform) – whilst actually pursuing their very own politics when negotiating with their stakeholders. Drawing on a micro-economist perfective, Rieder and Sire (2013) take Gillespie's argument further by outlining how platforms operate as multi-sided markets (Rochet & Tirole 2006), which offer the same product to a range of different actors, namely users, advertisers, media outlets, and other corporate partners. These accounts explore the functionalities platforms offer to their distinct stakeholder groups as key instances to a) address their needs and b) bring together their often divergent objectives. What is missing in this perspective are the socio-technical conditions that allow platforms to involve these stakeholders. In this paper, I claim that the most relevant condition for stakeholder involvement and programmability are the data-points of platforms, their pre-structured forms and flexibility in meaning. Take the case of Instagram, where users may be interested in creating and sharing images, advancing their social relations, engaging in interactions or building influence, whilst advertisers seek to identify, reach and engage relevant target audiences and brands set out to involve influencers as Instagram's business interface offers dedicated analytics for these aims.[1] Developers, on the contrary, are provided with extensive documentations on how to access platform data via application programming interfaces (APIs) and guidelines on how to use them.[2] All these interests are held together by the specific data Instagram and its stakeholders create, structure and recombine.

The divergent interests and valuation regimes of platform stakeholders do not have to be similar, nor align. Rather, the capacity of a well-functioning platform is to connect to a heterogeneous set of interests and/or valuation regimes. Indeed, Gillespie argues: "Consumers of online video are empowered to be their own content programmers, consuming the relevant mix of mass, niche and personal media they demand. Advertisers are empowered through data to better understand and engage with their audiences. And content owners are empowered, through sophisticated identification tools, to control their content and make smart

---

1   https://business.instagram.com
2   https://www.instagram.com/developer

business decisions with their content (Hurley, 2008)" (2010, 355). In order to advance their own profit and popularity, platforms need to enable stakeholders to pursue their respective interests, and in so doing, speak to what economic sociologists Boltanski and Thevenot (1991) posit as distinct orders of worth.

Boltanski and Thevenot are interested in valuation regimes in societies. They leave behind the differentiation between economic value and social values to focus on the more plural notion of worth. Therefore, they ask how people justify their action and reach agreements by taking on a pragmatist perspective that studies individual actors and their situated valuations. The authors start from the observation that the same object, issue or company can be viewed and valued differently according to specific valuation regimes or what they call "orders of worth." Each order, of which economic value is but only one, comes with distinct measures, metrics and justifications of value. The authors go on to explore how these orders can be used as means of orientation in situations of risk and uncertainty in order to reach agreements about the value of entities. Boltanski and Thevenot consult canonical philosophic texts to identify six orders of worth which include: inspired, domestic, fame, civic, market and industrial. Agreement about the value of goods, information/data, companies or processes can easily be reached when dealing with actors who operate according to the same order of worth, and is more difficult to achieve when conflicting orders are applied. The value of entities is thus determined relationally and is not fixed or stable.

When exploring the different stakeholders of platforms, divergent orders of worth can be detected – users seek to gain relational value and/or fame, activists may follow civic values, whilst advertisers and corporate partners follow market orders. What is interesting in the case of platforms is that these value formats do not necessary contradict each other or lead to fundamental dissent. Furthermore, so it shall be shown, these orders are not necessarily reliant on distinct actions, measures, metrics or indicators. The data and metrics offered to users and advertisers in their respective platform interfaces may be interpreted alongside different orders of worth: Likes on Facebook for instance can be treated as signifiers of social appreciation, cultural relevance or as indicators for successful promotion. Hashtags on Instagram can be used and interpreted as markers of association by users, as means to reach and build audiences for professional users, as campaigning tool for politicians or as demarcators of research samples for researchers. All these different interpretations and use cases speak to their distinct order of worth (domestic, fame oriented, inspired etc). What is distinct about social media is that the same data-points can operate in and be relevant for different valuation regimes as they can be interpreted differently. Whilst Boltanski and Thevenot address the capacity of entities to speak to different orders of worth as possible source of conflict, this may not necessarily the case in social media, as actors can interpret the same data differently here.

Such simultaneity of valuation regimes has been identified as central for innovation and growth by economic sociologist David Stark (2009). Whilst Boltanski and Thevenot have focused on the possibilities to achieve agreement between conflicting orders of worth, Stark suggests that a production friction that can arise when different orders of worth are in play can be productive and desirable. In his ethnographic fieldwork in different organisational settings, such as new media start-ups but also producing companies, he found that if different ideas of how to move forward, how to solve problems, or what a company should stand for exist, arriving at a solution to a problem may be longer and more conflictual as divergent valuation regimes prevent actors to come to an agreement. Such disagreement between valuation regime can lead to productive frictions that allow organisation to be become more inventive, agile and innovative as they do not settle on solutions too easily and explore problems from multiple perspectives. A multiplicity of valuation regimes in place allows employees to challenge established assumptions, to identify creative solutions to problems and thus to exploit uncertainty instead of being terrified by it. "[I]nviting more than one way of evaluating worth" (27), Stark agues, enables more open-ended forms of search that prevents organisations to settle on mediocre solutions. By so doing, he argues: "entrepreneurship is the ability to keep multiple principles of evaluation in play and to benefit from that productive friction" (Stark 2009: 9). He understand the simultaneity of different valuation regimes a "heterarchy" of worth and value. Central to a productive heterarchy of worth is firstly a form of "asset ambiguity", that is the possibility to view a situation or an entity from different valuation perspectives and secondly the constant re-evaluation of the same problem or entity based on different orders of worth, as "[v]alues mate to change" (181).

Operating as intermediaries of stakeholders who all follow their own agenda, it can be said that platforms enact such heterarchy, however in a more distributed and less bounded way. Whilst Stark focuses on the strategic invitation of conflicting orders of value within a single organisation, team or unit, platforms can only create the technical conditions and situations for such heterarchy to be enacted by its various stakeholders. The multiplicity of valuation regimes is not simply realised by the platform and its employees, but through assemblages of heterogeneous and previously disconnected stakeholders. In a next step, the paper will engage more with the socio-technical conditions for such heterarchy.

Infrastructures of valuation: standardised in form and flexible in meaning

To understand how these heterachies are made possible and are realised, it is not only relevant to focus on platform data in its given form, but the entire infrastructure of its making, organisation and circulation. The majority of platform data results from users engaging with platform features, such as posting images, following others, using hashtags, @mentions, captions, locations or filters, clicking on buttons, viewing profiles – to name only a few in the case of Instagram. These activities are enabled through pre-structured features which result into equally pre-structured data-points and associated meta-data.³ Data collection of platforms can therefore be understood as capture system in the sense of Philip Agre (1994). The information theorist explored how technologies create specific socio-technical conditions for monitoring activity and differentiated between two key models: surveillance and capture. Surveillance refers to modes of observation during which action and its monitoring are two separate acts. In a capture structure, on the contrary, action and its capture collapse, as actions are made possible by infrastructures that immediately track and transform action into predefined data formats. Both models have different origins: "Whereas the surveillance model originates in the classically political sphere of state action, the capture model has deep roots in the practical application of computer systems" (Agre 1994: 744). But capture systems can be applied to other fields, such as the standardisation of work processes in organisations, an example that Agre himself uses, and is, so this paper argues, central to social media platforms. Whenever users engage with a platform, their actions are not monitored retrospectively through modes of observation (surveillance) but recorded the moment the action occurs, as each action automatically generates an associated representation in a database. Capture structures are reliant on models of what users or in the case of Agre's object – organisations and their employers – can do. These models of desired behaviours are translated into a form of language consisting of words (that is actions) that can be combined into specific sentences or texts (that is action sequences). Agre understands these predefined possibilities to act as "grammars of action", which are enacted in a five step cycle.

First, existing or desired activity needs to be analysed and turned into an ideal-type model. Second, actions must be translated and categorised into grammatised, pre-structured forms. Third, these grammars need to be communicated, explained and made relevant to their potential users to enact compliance and to give the grammars a normative force. Fourth, grammars need to be turned into technical means or infrastructures that provide the technical conditions for grammatised action. In the context of platforms, step three and four cannot be separated as grammars can only gain a normative force if the technical means for their enactment, that is pre-structured platform actions, are provided. Fifth, the captured data enters a database and becomes amenable for further use, including the evaluation of the capture system, recombination with other data or – in the context of platforms – commercially motivated analysis of user preferences.

---

3   In addition, many platforms also draw on platform-external yet equally pre-structured data generated across the web (Helmond 2015a), such as shared content and associated responses or tracking devices build into social plugins which account for user actions and interest outside the platform by tracking their browsing behaviour (Gerlitz & Helmond 2013).

Agre's grammars of action thus have to be understood as socio-technical processes, as they require both technical infrastructures and user compliance. They are relevant to understand the making, use and valuation of platform data: User interfaces of platforms are also based on a set of modelled and desired possibilities to act, as imagined by platform designers – whether this be captions and hashtags on Instagram or posts, Likes and friend requests on Facebook, only to name a few. User action is only possible through such pre-structured grammars. Thus, users can Like on Instagram, but not Dislike, whilst on Facebook, they can select between different affective responses (Gerlitz et al. 2015). In the context of platforms, action outside of grammatised features is not possible and grammars take on a particularly normative as they "constitute a reorganization of the existing activity, as opposed to simply a representation of it" (Agre 1994: 747). Such normative force is central to social media, where platforms delineate the horizons of possible action (Langlois & Elmer 2013), offering some action in standardised form rather than another. Within these horizons, grammars can be more or less fine grained. In the context of Facebook's Like button, users have long requested an additional dislike feature to express negative reactions and have deployed the existing Like for multiple objectives – catering to forms of affective, ironic, attentive and other forms of liking, before the more differentiated response buttons where introduced.

Heterogeneous interpretations of technology are a long held topic in science and technology studies, as well as in valuation studies. Wiebe Bijker and Trevor Pinch (1984) for instance address the tensions between stabilisation and reinterpretation of technology as "interpretative flexibility". Technologies, the authors suggest, may have been designed with specific use cases or objectives in mind, but during certain stages of their development are open to be re-interpreted and re-purposed for different objectives. Facebook's Like Button for instance may have been designed as positive affective response, but has been deployed as in ironic or parodist ways or as means to negotiate relations or signal attention. Bijker and Pinch develop a dynamic account of technology which can be socially shaped and subject to different orders of worth. Drawing on the evolution of bicycles and cycling practices, the authors show how different developers have constantly reinterpreted what bicycles can do and how cycling can become part of everyday life before it took on its current form – or to put it with Bijker and Pinch – before cycling has stabilised. Key to their account are what they call "relevant social groups" involved in negotiating the use cases; meaning and value of technology; the wider social contest (or orders of worth); and the stabilisation or closure of interpretative flexibility once technologies are used in standardised ways. The authors are particularly interested in how the negotiation between stakeholders may lead to a closure of the interpretative flexibility and how standardised use scenarios and valuation regimes are established.

The notion of interpretative flexibility offers a relevant framing when studying how users adopt to or re-interpret grammatised actions in the context of platforms.

Recent social media research has started to engage with the concept of interpretative flexibility, but mainly in relation to platforms as a whole such as exploring the stabilisation and flexibility of Twitter (Dijck 2013b) or YouTube (Burgess 2014). By looking at the structural elements of platforms, their technicity, stakeholders and practices, it is difficult, if not impossible to speak of the stabilisation of an entire platform – that is claiming that Twitter only stands for real-time live commentary, Facebook is only used for keeping in contact with one's existing network of friends and LinkedIn for professional network building. Rather than exploring the interpretation of a platform as a whole, I suggest to draw attention to the interpretative flexibility of individual grammars and their entanglement with the valuation dynamics of platforms. Take the case of Twitter and its former Favourite and now Like button, a largely disregarded feature (Paßmann & Gerlitz 2014).[4] The majority of users have deployed Favourites in the same way as bookmarks to save interesting tweets; but sub-groups, particularly present on German and US Twitter, have used the Favourite as a signal of social appreciation and recognition.[5] Third party developers realised these complementary interpretations and offered complementary services such as bookmarking apps to save Favourites, or popularity rankings for the most 'fav'ed' accounts and tweets – as in the case of Favstar. The various social groups involved in Twitter thus rendered the Favourite subject to interpretative flexibility. The transformation of Favourites to Likes in November 2015, however, interfered with this interpretative flexibility although the platform likes to tell a different story (Gerlitz et al. 2015). As Favourites are now presented as a heart, journalists for instance felt that they cannot use it as bookmark as easily as before, as they did not want to save tweets from terrorists or about catastrophes by giving them a heart. The previous Favourite button was considered to be more open to interpretative flexibility than the new Twitter Like which may have introduced a partial closure to the possible value registers alongside which the button can be used. In short, the feature was perceived to cater to a heterarchy of valuation regimes until it was transformed into a Like button. Bijker and Pinch's notion of interpretative flexibility draws attention to the dynamics between flexibility and closure and the involvement of various social groups who negotiate this relationship. How these groups are entangled through the above discussed capture and grammar systems and whether a closure of interpretative flexibility is aimed for by these groups will be the focus of the next sections.

---

4   For a detailed history of Twitter features, see Paßmann 2016.
5   See Ian Bogost's taxonomy of the Twitter Favourite here https://twitter.com/ibogost/status/603231455804858370

Back-end grammatisation

In the context of platforms, a variety of stakeholders are involved in the negotiation of interpretative flexibility of platform grammars. As discussed elsewhere (Gerlitz & Rieder 2015), platforms are informed by different levels of grammatisation and whilst users encounter their grammars through pre-structured platform actions, developers and analysts are facing specific back-end grammars via application programming interfaces (APIs) that allow to input or output platform data through a series of grammatised API commands. Instagram offers a developer API[6] and an advertising API via Facebook[7]. Once developers have authorised to gain access, they can retrieve data through pre-structured lines of code, connecting themselves to the so-called API end-points for data input and output[8]. Like other platforms, Instagram provides an extensive library that lists all possible data formats that can be retrieved by predefined API commands which I suggest to understand as back-end grammars (Gerlitz & Rieder 2015). It is for instance possible to automatically extract all media posted from a given area, posts tagged with selected keywords or liked by specific users. APIs are designed for both data retrieval and to build alternative interfaces for sharing and creating content. To cater to these two objectives, platform APIs usually come with so called GET grammars for data extraction, and POST grammars to act or create new content. These back-end grammars largely resonate with the front-end grammars, as (a) they rely on the data produced by front-end grammars and (b) produce content that is being made visible in front-ends as well. However, especially GET grammars may extend the ways in which data can be accessed or searched in the front-ends by offering new means of aggregation.

Back-end grammars of platforms can be subject to the interpretative flexibility of diverse stakeholder groups: they can be used for data extraction for business analytics or to build new apps on top of the platform, like photo editors or download apps for Instagram. Platforms are reliant on their diverse stakeholders to explore the potentials of the platforms and possible interpretations of its feature in order to generate new incentives for users to engage, to innovate platform development or to create new models of economic valorisation (Halavais 2014). On the other hand, back-end grammars may be subject to even more interpretative flexibility than front-end grammars as they allow to re-interpret the meaning of grammatised action and to recombine data alongside new valuation regimes – that is to use it for forecasting, popularity rankings, controversy mapping or user profiling. Therefore, back-end grammars are often more closely watched and guided by platforms (Bucher 2013) through extensive sets of rules and strategy plans that define which types of interpretation of back-end grammars are supported by the

---

6 https://www.instagram.com/developer/
7 https://developers.facebook.com/docs/marketing-api/guides/instagramads
8 https://www.instagram.com/developer/endpoints/

platform and which not. In late 2015, Instagram announced a stricter app review procedure and announced it would only support apps who adhere to the following three development aims: (1) enable "individuals to share their own content with 3rd party apps", (2) support "brands and advertisers understand, manage their audience and media rights" and (3) "help broadcasters and publishers discover content, get digital rights to media, and share media with proper attribution".[9] All apps were made subject to a strict review process and their access to Instagram's API data was discontinued if they did not follow one of these three aims. With these guidelines, Instagram deliberately terminated its support for apps that offer alternative Instagram viewers or interfaces to one's feed and caused problems to many research oriented apps[10]. Therefore, the introduction of the guidelines was perceived as "platform cleanup" (Brennan 2015) in the development community and can be accounted for as partial closure of the interpretative flexibility of back-end grammars. Grammatisation in front- and back-ends, as well as access points to data for developers form the infrastructures that enable different stakeholders to pursue their interests. The standardisation in form and flexibility in meaning allows different stakeholders to interpret platform data to fit their very own meaning without necessarily having to achieve an agreement between their orders of worth.

Enacting the multivalence of platform data

The question emerges how various stakeholders of platforms have made use of and negotiated their freedoms and how users and other stakeholders can engage with their interpretations. As a comprehensive study would exceed the limits of this paper, I will only outline the contours of a methodological experiment conducted in the context of a Digital Methods Winter School at the University of Amsterdam in 2016 lead together with Anne Helmond, Fernando van der Vlist, Esther Weltevrede and others.[11] This experiment does not allow to map all interpretations and valuations of platform data by relevant stakeholders, but offers insight into a very significant section of them, namely apps that are built on top of a platform and that

---

9   https://www.instagram.com/developer/
10 http://thepoliticsofsystems.net/2016/05/closing-apis-and-the-public-scrutiny-of-very-large-online-platforms/
11 The experiment has its origin in the 2016 Digital Methods Winter School, where a group of researchers, students, programmers, journalists and designers facilitated by Anne Helmond, Fernando van der Vlist, Esther Weltevrede and me explored the interpretation of platform features and metrics through third-party apps. For an overview of the project results, see the presentation https://docs.google.com/presentation/d/1aC6IPPF8vy-ThPS6PjvaumGtIds7lOIjS96BsQJTWZk/edit?pref=2&pli=1#slide=id.p

make use of its grammatised data through APIs, or apps that help users engaging with platforms without necessarily directly connecting to its data. Doing so, the exercise can provide an experimental and partial view into a set of stakeholders, namely developers and third party companies that set out to explore the interpretative flexibility of platform data and their value.

The visualisation below shows a network of apps built by recombining Instagram data or created to enhance the use of Instagram. As users mainly search for and engage with new apps in the respective app stores for Android or iOS, the experiment used the search and similar app function of the Google Play Store to identify these apps and their relations. In a first step, the Play Store was queried for the respective platform, here Instagram. Instagram was selected as example due to its rich third party development ecosystem. Then, all apps suggested as similar by the store for the top 100 results for the query Instagram were identified. These similar apps are not exclusive and the apps can share similar apps in the Play Store. The data was systematically extracted by the Google Play Similar Apps tool developed by the Digital Methods Initiative[12] which detects similar apps and turns the findings into data formats amenable for network visualisation. The visualisation was created with the open-source network visualisation tool Gephi.[13] The nodes show all apps identified as connected to Instagram and the edges, that is the connections between the nodes, show which apps are considered similar to each other. It is important to note that a categorisation of the apps in the network showed that 82% apps support users in their engagement with Instagram and 18% only offer services that are similar to that of Instagram, but are not reuse Instagram data. The result is a variety of clusters of topically related apps, that take up Instagram data and features in order to enhance, alter or re-interpret them. The network allows to pose the question alongside which valuation regimes do developers repurpose and re-interpret Instagram data and features. The colour of the clusters results from Gephi's modularity algorithm which detects nodes (in this case apps) that are particularly closely connected. For further orientation, I annotated outlined five thematically focused clusters of apps that stand out through their shared engagement and valuation of Instagram data.

A first cluster of apps offers users means to reinterpret their relations to friends and followers in strategic and popularity oriented ways. This clusters entails apps that support follower and popularity management for users, including follower analytics ("Follower Stats/Insight for Instagram", "FollowMeter for Instagram"), follower growth apps ("free followers", "Real Followers for Instagram") or apps showing who viewed one's posts ("Who viewed your Instagram"). These apps redeploy Instagram data to offer users additional analytics, tips or action possibilities to approach their followers in a strategic way following both a fame and market oriented order of worth. A second cluster takes up existing platform grammars

---

12 https://tools.digitalmethods.net/beta/googlePlaySimilar/ developed by Erik Borra.
13 https://gephi.org/

and enhances them to support different interpretations and thus valuations of them. Here, hashtag related apps figure most central. On the one hand, hashtags can be used to create topical associations of posts in the caption, on the other hand, they function as key search device on Instagram as users can only finds new content based on hashtags and location. A lot of apps thus reinterpret hashtags as means to strategically connect to audiences and gain likes by offering randings or collections of most popular hashtags, such as "TopTags" or "HashTags". Hence, hashtags can be deployed alongside various orders of worth: to describe posts in inventive and creative ways, for civic engagement or to optimise hashtag use for strategic popularity growth.

A third cluster focuses at expanding the possibilities to engage with Instagram beyond its pre-structured grammars. Apps like "InstaSaver" or "InstaSave for Instagram" allow users to perform actions that exceed platform grammars, such as downloading or saving Instagram content to re-use it for one's own purposes outside of the platform. Other apps we examined show who has viewed one's images, such as the aforementioned "Who viewed your Instagram" app, again providing stats that are not available on Instagram itself. Another action enabled by third party apps is reposting – a feature that Instagram deliberately does not offer to incentivise users to create their own content instead of re-posting other people's images. The lack of a repost-grammar has led to the development of workarounds, for instance by screenshotting content, manually cropping and posting it – often at the expense of crediting the source. Various repost apps allow to skip the screenshoot-and-crop part by offering one-click solutions which also credit sources ("Repost for Instagram" or "Insta Repost for Instagram"). Apps in this cluster aim to expand the existing front-end grammars by making inventive use of back-end grammars. Especially in the case of reposting, they cut across Instagram's valuation of original content by allowing for one-click sharing possibilities.

A fourth cluster concerned images and photo editing. Here we saw 'workarounds' to Instagram's previous limitation to only square images. These apps enabled alternative modes of viewing and compiling pictures, for instance into collages ("Photo Grid: Photo Collage Maker" or "InstaSquare Size Pic Collage"). Moreover, the photo editing clusters comprised of many beauty and selfie focused editors, such as "Selfie Camera – InstaBeauty" which allow users to retouch their selfies. This cluster was partially aimed at re-interpreting constraints Instagram put on user grammars, namely the fact that users for a long time could only post square images and support users to deploy the platform for their own objectives including self-presentation and self-aesthetisation. The final cluster concerned videos on Instagram in the widest sense, from video editing apps such as "Video Editor Music,Cut,No Crop", video collage makers like "Video Collage for Instagram" or various video downloaders like "Video Downloader for Instagram". These collage makers can all be understood as re-interpretating Instagram's grammars by offering means to view and recombine Instagram content in alternative ways and to repurpose it outside of the platform.

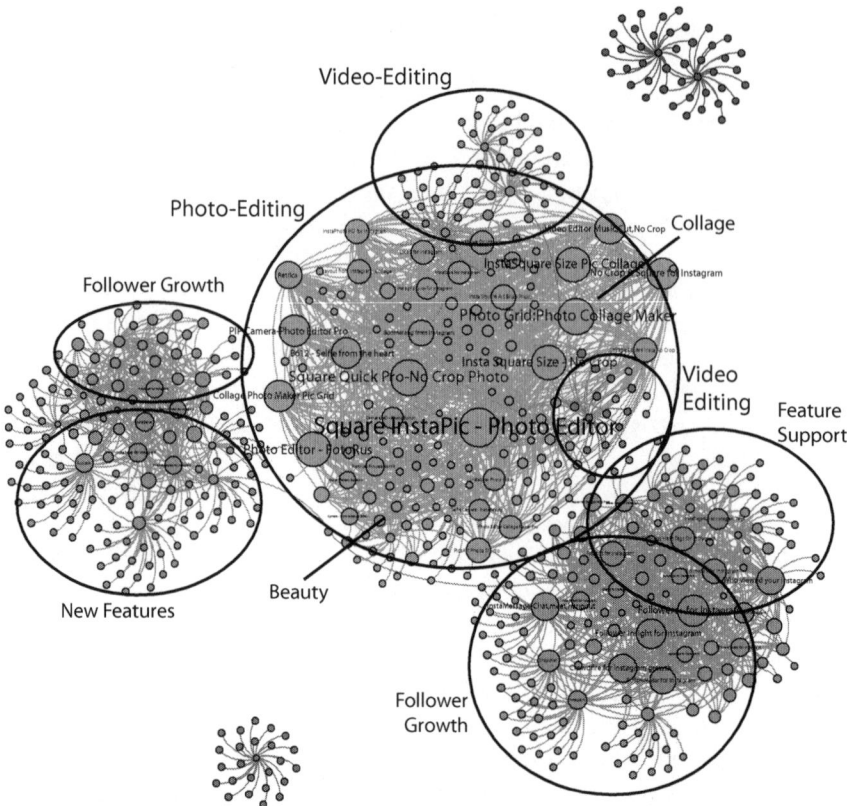

Image 1: Support app network for Instagram based on Google Play Store (Sept. 2016).

The apps identified in this experiment all focus on supporting, expanding, or re-interpreting the platform's features and data. What is striking is the lack of thematically oriented apps, assembling Instagram content regarding specific topics like food, sports or politics. Instead we encountered apps that contribute to render Instagram features and data multi-valent as they re-interpret them alongside different valuation regimes. Apps allow follower relations to be reorganised in strategic ways, allows hashtags to be used to maximise popularity and exposure and offer photo editors who support self-presentation. Developers thus draw on different interpretations of what users can do with platform features and data and cater to these diverse objectives. Just as the platform itself, these apps only offer the technical conditions for such valuation as they need to be engaged with and realised by users – a perspective that this experiment cannot cover. Despite its limitations, this experimental mapping indicates that the various stakeholders involved in platforms indeed contribute to deploy its back-end grammars for valuation alongside a multiplicity of valuation regimes. The potential multi-valence of platform features and data is thus enacted in a distributed way that enables users, third party developers and the platform itself to participate in the re-interpretation and valuation of platform grammars. Programmability, stakeholder involvement and valuation emerge as key conditions and drivers of the third-party app market. However, Instagram's app ecosystem largely complies to the strategic aims of apps Instagram set out to support – as alternative feed reader and viewing apps have not been found. The question emerges whose interpretations of the platform count and what the conditions for participating in the valuation of platform data are.

What counts and who counts?

This paper set out to develop an account of valuation processes of platform data and sought to expand the characteristics of social media platforms by focusing on the valuation of platform data. Platforms, it has been argued throughout the paper, enable specific socio-technical conditions for data valuation. The key characteristics of platforms identified by previous research, namely programmability, affordances, constraints and the involvement of heterogeneous stakeholders on the one hand lay the foundation for the valuation of data alongside multiple orders or worth. On the other hand, the interplay of these characteristics can be considered to be fuelled by valuation processes, as the ways in which different stakeholders approach and enact the programmability of platforms is very much informed by their valuation objectives.

The paper put forward the claim that platform data is produced to become multivalent. It is created by capture infrastructures and engaged with through various predefined grammars in both front-ends and back-ends, each speaking to distinct stakeholders. Front-end grammars may be pre-structured in form, but are flexible in their meaning and users do engage with them following different interpretations and objectives, which, in the end, all result into the same standardised data format. These data formats can then be engaged with through respective back-end grammars by developers which further interpret the data following their own valuation regimes. Such multivalence of platform data is made possible as grammatisation allows data to be pre-structured in form and flexible in interpretation and valuation. Different than in the development of technological standards, platforms not necessarily strive to close the interpretative flexibility of their data and features but are reliant on it for their own distributed development.

The fact that platform data can speak to multiple orders of worth is, however, neither specific to social media nor to contemporary economic valuation in general, but needs to be located in regards to post-Fordist modes of value production operating since the 1970s, which derive value from cultural and social domains outside of economic production by "putting life to work" (Lazzarato 2004: 205; Boltanski & Chiapello 2006). What is specific to platforms, however, are the ways in which platforms create the socio-technical conditions for multivalence that allow their data to operate across multiple orders of worth. Whilst Boltanski and Thevenot notify the existence of (potentially conflicting) orders of worth, they claim that each order of worth comes with its own specific measures, metrics and bounded infrastructures. In the case of platforms, however, the same metrics – namely the same grammatised features and data-points – and the same infrastructures – namely APIs and their back-end grammars – potentially serve to multiple orders or worth. A hashtag can be used for diverse objectives – to connect to friends, ironically, strategically, for commercial data analysis, for strategic follower growth or for politically motivated issue analysis. The pre-structuredness in form and openness in interpretation allow platform data to participate in multiple orders of value.

Multivalence in the context of platforms further differs from Boltanski and Thevenot's notion as the orders of worth at stake in platforms do not require exclusivity or agreement. Pre-structured data can be part of conflicting or mal-aligned orders of value at the very same time without necessarily interfering in the respective valuation processes. To understand how data can simultaneously participate in multiple orders of worth, the notion of partibility and partible persons developed by ethnographer Marilyn Strathern (1988) becomes relevant. Partible persons may be detached from one context, set of relations or value regimes and connected to another, yet remain partly attached to their origin. In the process of partial detachment, the person remains connected to its origin whilst also being connected to the new context. The value of social media data can be understood as partible in a similar way. Whilst users may interpret hashtags or followings in their own specific ways, the grammatisation and capture of their actions render all divergent interpretations into the same data format which can then be reinterpreted again by apps alongside new orders of worth – while remaining its original partible connections to users and their interpretations. Just because third parties deploy Likes to calculate the popularity of topics, does not mean that the specific Like a user received ceases to have social and relational value for that user. The value of the data lies both partly with the actor who produced the data, the platform which relies on this data and the various stakeholders who detach and re-attach the data to new valuation regimes. It is partibly distributed across the different actors involved. The value of social media data is not a property but a capacity that needs to be enacted in social and distributed ways (see also Lury & Marres 2014). In that sense, data can be included in various orders of worth but does not belong to them in exclusive ways. Drawing on Adrian Mackenzies' work on relational databases (2012), it can be argued that social media data faces an excess of inclusion (or participation) over belonging: "No one belongs to a database as element, but many aspects of contemporary lives are included as parts of databases" (342). Just as databases are set up as infrastructures facilitating the inclusion of datapoints into new sets of relations, platform infrastructures are set out to incentivise developers to include their data into new orders of worth.

But the question of participation can also be addressed the other way around – whilst data can potentially participate and be organised alongside different orders of worth, can all stakeholders participate in these multiple processes of valuation as well? Previous work on platforms already outlined that it is the platform which creates the conditions of participation through its politics (Gillespie 2010), for instance by regulating access to APIs (Bucher 2013; Puschmann & Burgess 2014) or determining which third-party apps will be supported. Platforms like Instagram accompany their back-end grammars with a series of desired strategic aims – that is orders of worth – and deploy extended documentations or review processes to ensure compliance to their policy.[14] As addressed before, Instagram decided to discontinue support for alternative Instagram readers in late 2015, impacting apps like "Gramfeed" or "Mixagram". This decision allowed Instagram to ensure users would more likely view content on their official interface and can therefore be exposed to paid content or advertising better. Furthermore, Instagram required apps to use access tokens to query for hashtags.[15] Hashtag aggregators that create rankings and collections of most popular hashtags would now require users to log into the app with their Instagram account to retrieve hashtags – which adds an additional access barrier. This may come with consequences for the widely popular hashtag analysis apps discussed above and may result into a partial closure of the interpretative flexibility of this grammar in order to enable the platform to pursue its own orders of worth. A heterarchy of valuation regimes is possible in the context of social media platforms, as long as the platform itself can realise its valuation aims.

This paper set out to establish multivalence as key characteristic of platform data and its process of production, organisation and recombination. Valuation has emerged as dynamic and distributed process in the context of platforms and value cannot be considered as property of platform data, but as a capacity of data and the socio-technical conditions of its making. Platform data can potentially participate in multiple orders of worth that have to be realised by different stakeholders deploying the programmability of platforms. A critical account on platforms thus needs to attend to the generative and restrictive politics of platforms and interpretative actions of various stakeholders that enable platform data to participate in different orders of worth – or not. Extensive empirical work is needed to create precise accounts on the enactment of orders of worth and such work also needs to attend to the role of platform networks – as corporations like Facebook or Google own various platforms and can also interoperate grammatised data among them. Understanding the distributed socio-technical conditions of valuation and their specific and situated enactment poses the foundation for devising alternative accounts of 'what counts'.

---

14   https://www.instagram.com/about/legal/terms/api/
15   https://www.dialogfeed.com/update-instagram-api-changes-restrictions-solutions/

References

Agre, Philip E. (1994): "Data Derivatives: On the Emergence of a Security Risk Calculus for Our Times." In: Theory, Culture & Society 28/6, pp. 24–43.

Bell, Emily (2015): "Twitter's Heart Hits the Wrong Beat." In: The Guardian, 9 November (https://www.theguardian.com/media/2015/nov/08/twitter-heart-wrong-beat).

Bijker, Wiebe E./Hughes, Thomas P./Pinch, Trevor F. (eds.) (1987): The Social Construction of Technological Systems. New Directions in the Sociology and History of Technology, Cambridge, MA: MIT Press.

Bogost, Ian/Montfort, Nick (2009): "The New Spirit of Capitalism." International Journal of Politics, Culture, and Society 18/3-4, pp. 161–188.

Boltanski, Luc/Thevenot, Laurent (1991): On Justification. Economies of Worth, Princeton: Princeton University Press.

Borra, Erik/Weber, Ingmar (2012): "Political Insights: Exploring Partisanship in Web Search Queries." In: First Monday 17/7.

boyd, danah/Crawford, Kate (2011): "Six Provocations for Big Data." In: A Decade in Internet Time: Symposium on the Dynamics of the Internet and Society, September 2011 (http://ssrn.com/abstract=1926431).

Brennan, Martin W. (2015): "Instagram Shuts Down Feed API as Part of Platform Cleanup." In: ProgrammableWeb, 10 May (http://www.programmableweb.com/news/instagram-shuts-down-feed-api-part-platform-cleanup/brief/2015/11/19).

Bruns, Axel/Stieglitz, Stefan (2013): "Towards More Systematic Twitter Analysis: Metrics for Tweeting Activities." In: International Journal of Social Research Methodology 16/2, pp. 91–108.

Bucher, Taina (2013): "Objects of Intense Feeling: The Case of the Twitter." In: Computational Culture 3.

Burgess, Jean (2014): "From 'Broadcast Yourself' to 'Follow Your Interests': Making over Social Media." In: International Journal of Cultural Studies 18/3.

Collins, H. M. (1975): "The Seven Sexes: A Study in the Sociology of a Phenomenon, or the Replication of Experiments in Physics." In: Sociology 9/2, pp. 205–224.

Dewey, John (1969): Theory of Valuation, Chicago: University of Chicago Press.

Gerlitz, Carolin (2012). Brands and Continuous Economies, Goldsmiths/University of London: PhD dissertation (https://research.gold.ac.uk/9466/1/SOC_thesis_Gerlitz_2013.pdf).

Gerlitz, Carolin/Helmond, Anne (2013): "The Like Economy – Social Buttons and the Data-Intensive Web." In: New Media & Society 15/8, pp. 1348–1365.

Gerlitz, Carolin/Herma, Leonie/Kyrimi, Christina Giannouli (2015): "The Disambiguation of Social Buttons." In: POP-Zeitschrift (http://www.pop-zeitschrift.de/2015/11/16/social-media-november/).

Gerlitz, Carolin/Rieder, Bernhard (2015): Tweets Are Not Created Equal. The Politics of Platform Metrics, Manuscript.

Gillespie, Tarleton (2010): "The Politics of 'Platforms.'" In: New Media & Society 12/3, pp. 347–364.

Graeber, David (2006): "Value: Anthropological Theories of Value." In: James G. Carrier (ed.): A Handbook of Economic Anthropology, Northampton, MA: Edward Elgar, pp. 439–454.

Hearn, Alison (2010): "Structuring Feeling: Web 2.0, Online Ranking and Rating, and the Digital 'reputation' Economy." In: ephemera 10/3-4, pp. 421–438.

Helmond, Anne (2015): "The Platformization of the Web: Making Web Data Platform Ready." In: Social Media + Society 1/2, pp. 1–11.

Keating, Peter/Cambrosio, Alberto (2003): Biomedical Platforms: Realigning the Normal and the Pathological in Late-Twentieth-Century Medicine, Cambridge, MA: MIT Press.

Langlois, Ganaele/Elmer, Greg (2013): "The Research Politics of Social Media Platforms." In: Culture Machine 14, pp. 1–17.

Lazzarato, Maurizio (2004): "From Capital-Labour to Capital-Life." In: ephemera 4/3, pp. 187–208.

Lury, Celia/Marres, Noortje (2014): Notes on Objectual Valuation, Manuscript.

Mackenzie, Adrian (2012): "More Parts than Elements: How Databases Multiply." In: Environment and Planning D: Society and Space 30/2, pp. 335–350.

Marres, Noortje/Moats, David (2015): "Mapping Controversies with Social Media: The Case for Symmetry." In: Social Media + Society 1/2.

Marres, Noortje (2011): "The Costs of Public Involvement. Everyday Devices of Carbon Accounting and the Materialisation of Participation." In: Economy and Society, 40/4, pp. 510–533.

Moor, Liz/Lury, Celia (2011): "Making and Measuring Value. Comparison, Singularity and Agency in Brand Valuation Practice." In: Journal of Cultural Economy 4/4, pp. 439–454.

Paßmann, Johannes (2016): Was war Twitter? Eine Medien-Ethnographie, University of Siegen: PhD dissertation.

Paßmann, Johannes/Gerlitz, Carolin (2014): "'Good' Platform-Political Reasons for 'Bad' Platform-Data. Zur Sozio-Technischen Geschichte der Plattformaktivitäten Fav, Retweet und Like." In: Mediale Kontrolle unter Beobachtung 3/1, pp. 1–40.

Pinch, Trevor J./Bijker, Wiebe E. (1984): "The Social Construction of Facts and Artefacts: Or How the Sociology of Science and the Sociology of Technology Might Benefit Each Other." In: Social Studies of Science 14/3, pp. 399–441.

Puschmann, Cornelius/Burgess, Jean (2014): "The Politics of Twitter Data." In: Katrin Weller/Axel Bruns/Jean Burgess/Merja Mahrt/Cornelius Puschmann (eds.): Twitter and Society, New York et al.: Peter Lang, pp. 43–54.

Rieder, Bernhard/Sire, Guillaume (2013): "Conflicts of Interest and Incentives to Bias: A Microeconomic Critique of Google's Tangled Position on the Web." In: New Media & Society 16/2, pp. 195–211.

Rochet, Jean-Charles/Tirole, Jean (2006): "Two-Sided Markets: A Progress Report." In: The RAND Journal of Economics 37/3, pp. 645–667.

Stark, David (2009): The Sense of Dissonance. Accounts of Worth in Economic Life, Princeton: Princeton University Press.

Strathern, Marilyn (1988): The Gender of the Gift: Problems With Women and Problems With Society in Melanesia, Berkeley: University of California Press.

Turow, Joseph (2006): Niche Envy: Marketing Discrimination in the Digital Age, Cambridge, MA: MIT Press.

Turow, Joseph (2012): The Daily You: How the New Advertising Industry Is Defining Your Identity and Your Worth, New Haven: Yale University Press.

van Dijck, José (2013b): "Tracing Twitter: The Rise of a Microblogging Platform." In: International Journal of Media and Cultural Politics 7, pp. 333–348.

van Dijck, Jose (2012): The Culture of Connectivity. A Critical History of Social Media, Oxford: Oxford University Press.

Vatin, François (2013): "Valuation as Evaluating and Valorizing." In: Valuation Studies 1/1, pp. 31–50.

Big Data and the Paradox of Diversity

Bernhard Rieder

Abstract

This paper develops a critique of Big Data and associated analytical techniques by focusing not on errors – skewed or imperfect datasets, false positives, underrepresentation, and so forth – but on data mining that works. After a quick framing of these practices as interested readings of reality, I address the question of how data analytics and, in particular, machine learning reveal and operate on the structured and unequal character of contemporary societies, installing "economic morality" (Allen 2012) as the central guiding principle. Rather than critiquing the methods behind Big Data, I inquire into the way these methods make the many differences in decentred, non-traditional societies knowable and, as a consequence, ready for profitable distinction and decision-making. The objective, in short, is to add to our understanding of the "profound ideological role at the intersection of sociality, research, and commerce" (van Dijck 2014: 201) the collection and analysis of large quantities of multifarious data have come to play. Such an understanding needs to embed Big Data in a larger, more fundamental critique of the societal context it operates in.

Keywords: Big data; analytical techniques; digital methods; data analysis; data mining.

Introduction

The emergence of Big Data, both as an imminent potentiality and an actual practice, has fuelled considerable discussion of possible social ramifications, ranging from the loss of privacy to the detrimental consequences of statistical bias. The latter aspect, in particular, highlights the implications of statistical models and decision rules learned from datasets that can be skewed or deficient in various ways. Sweeney (2013), for example, shows how racial bias manifests in ad delivery and Barocas/Selbst (2016) list various ways in which discrimination can creep into data mining to produce "disparate impact". An edited volume on *Discrimination and Privacy in the Information Society* (Custers et al. 2013) constitutes the so far most comprehensive effort to bring together computer scientists and legal scholars to investigate issues raised by data mining and consider possible solutions.

These works highlight the subtle intricacies involved in decision-making[1] that relies on data analysis techniques, which are not only conceptually difficult to apprehend due to their reliance on advanced mathematics, but also practically daunting, in the sense that decision models are not directly designed by a human agent, but derived from the iterative parsing of large quantities of complex and often problematic data. A growing body of work in the humanities and social sciences (cf. Kitchin 2016) has begun to highlight how algorithms intervene in various domains, although the specific operating principles that underpin algorithmic decisions remain elusive and hard to integrate into a vocabulary of agency designed to capture human conduct and reasoning.

At the same time, we witness not only the integration of algorithmic filtering, classification, and recommendation into the fabric of our digital environments, but also the intensification of a long-standing trend in commerce and government to turn to *empirical*, data-driven procedures that heavily rely on measurement and counting to make – and justify – decisions (cf. Porter 1995). In many areas of organizational life, we can see the development and application of approaches that set out to make Hume's (1739) famous consternation with the jump from an *is*, a description, to an *ought*, a prescription, somewhat less distressful. Cost-benefit analysis, evidence-based practice, data-driven government, impact analysis, and many other approaches promise to reconcile the tension between the increasingly accepted moral imperatives of impartiality, fairness, transparency, and accountability on the one side, and, on the other, the factual necessity to make decisions that will impact some people differently than others and thus participate in picking winners and losers. The turn to the empirical – through data collection and analysis – as arbiter is certainly not uncontested as the continuing disputes over global warming or vaccination indicate, but to place *ideology* over *evidence* has become a sure-fire way to get shunned from the community of the rational and reasonable – only the ignorant und unenlightened tune out the facts. At the same time, the "new spirit of capitalism" (Boltanski/Chiapello 1999) may have replaced the rigidities of Taylorist scientific management with principles such as flexibility, enthusiasm, and collaboration, but the associated embrace of uncertainty and probabilistic reasoning has led to *more* empiricism, not less.

This paper approaches Big Data practices as empiricism *on steroids* and develops a critique built around the idea that data analysis is more often than not applied to produce actionable forms of knowledge that are used "as tools for assessment, action, and decision" (Desrosières 2001: 344) instead of disinterested description. This critique deviates from the more common repudiations of Big Data's claims to objectivity (cf. Kitchin 2014) by situating data analysis and associ-

---

1   The term decision-making is often used in psychology, cognitive science, and behavioral economics to denote the selection between alternative beliefs or courses of action. My use of the term follows this general definition without necessarily subscribing to the larger theoretical frameworks it is usually embedded in.

ated practices in an epistemological paradigm that is informed by the purposes and ideas of the business world rather than modelled upon the predicates of scientific inquiry. Ad targeting techniques may not be able to *know* a user in any meaningful sense of the word, but they are clearly capable of producing higher clickthrough rates. Assessing Big Data from the angle of its effectiveness in delivering advantageous outcomes rather than its capacity to yield descriptive truth moves the space of potential issues from (broken) epistemic promises to everyday practices of social sorting and, consequently, questions of social justice (Lyon 2003).

These issues are certainly not unfamiliar, but, as I want to argue, Big Data raises them anew and with a twist. However, this paper also departs from broader, more comprehensive critiques (cf. Ekbia et al. 2014) by largely leaving aside the many issues stemming from deficiencies or inaccuracies in data analytics – skewed or imperfect datasets, false positives, underrepresentation, and so forth – to focus on data mining that *works*. Not that these issues are not important, on the contrary. But there is also need for more theoretical inquiries into the epistemic character of Big Data, into the ways of knowing it aspires to, and into its relationship with the dominant normative horizon of contemporary western societies. The objective, in short, is to add to our understanding of the "profound ideological role at the intersection of sociality, research, and commerce" (van Dijck 2014: 201) the collection and analysis of large quantities of multifarious data have come to play. After a quick framing of these practices as *interested* readings of reality, I will therefore focus on the question of how data analytics and, in particular, machine learning reveal and operate on the structured and unequal character of contemporary societies, highlighting "economic morality [as a] guiding logic that conditions and directs our daily lives" (Allen 2012: 19).

Big Data

To begin the argument, it is necessary to outline the technological context, space of application, and normative background I will be referring to throughout this text. There are numerous definitions of Big Data and associated techniques, but for the purpose of this paper, four elements are crucial.

First, we witness the steadily increasing production and availability of very large datasets that often comprise transactional data (logged behaviour) or other forms of non-traditional data such as social interactions, cultural tastes, or sensor readings.

Second, algorithmic techniques for data analysis, many of them probabilistic and capable of *learning*[2], have become widely available. Code libraries for various programming languages, easy-to-use analytics software, and integrated data

---

2   It should be noted that machine learning implements a specific and partial theory of learning that boils down to forms of statistical induction.

infrastructures offer sophisticated methods to mine vast amounts of stored data at high speeds and from diverse perspectives in the context of a quickly growing set of applications.

Third, the rampant computerization[3] of all aspects of contemporary life means that ever more practices are unfolding in online environments that allow for data collection as well as for the automation of decision-making and the performative implementation of its results. Differential pricing on the web provides an elucidating example: a user's location, software environment, browsing behaviour, and other elements can be situated against a horizon of millions of other users and their shopping behaviour; this knowledge can then be used to set the sales price of an item to the highest level the user has been estimated to support. The result of this calculation, made in the fraction of a second, can then be directly integrated in the interface served to that user, showing an individualized[4] price for an item. This instant *applicability* of data analysis is a crucial step beyond traditional uses of statistics because it integrates and automates the sequence of collecting data, making decisions, and applying results, thereby relegating human discretion to the design and control stages. As a consequence, the scope of data-driven techniques has been continuously extended from bureaucratic management into areas such as information ordering, real-time credit assessment, product pricing, or cultural recommendation.

Fourth, and more broadly, the relentless drift in economic and social organization towards market forms makes techniques that can adapt to and control complex and dynamic situations increasingly attractive. Especially in settings where largely autonomous actors cooperate and compete in shared informational infrastructures, such as online environments, fast, yet informed decisions are rewarded. Paraphrasing Andrejevic (2013), one could argue that algorithms are seen as the go-to solution whenever there is "too much": too many people and things, too much information, and, of course, too little time. This seems to apply to more and more areas of contemporary life, from business and government to the various online platforms that heavily rely on filtering, recommendation, and aggregation.

In addition to these four elements, a broader aspect I have already mentioned needs to be emphasised, namely that "[j]udgment and discretion, normally the prerogatives of elites, are discredited" (Porter 1995: 97), particularly in domains where (social) trust is eroding. Choosing a particular course of action based on

---

3   While the term has fallen out of fashion, it is highly useful to shift the focus to the computer – and not just its digital code – as the fundamental technological component of our "information societies".

4   A recent report by the White House summarizes: "Broadly speaking, big data seems likely to produce a shift from third-degree price discrimination based on broad demographic categories towards personalized pricing and individually targeted marketing campaigns." (Executive Office of the President of the United States 2015: 19)

the analysis of empirical data is by no means a new phenomenon in business and government. But even in mature, impersonal bureaucracies, these processes are riddled with moments of human discretion in the sense that managers and administrators interpret results and have a level of leeway when it comes to deciding how to proceed. This residual element of volition in moving from *is* to *ought* has been coming under scrutiny in areas where individual authority is perceived or portrayed as inadequate, inefficient, partial, paternalistic, corrupt, or illegitimate. In these areas, fully formalized, automated decisions have become more and more attractive as effective and supposedly neutral or even democratic procedures, in particular if they implement an empirical component that can be presented as "carrying" the actual decision. Responsibility can then be shifted to the data themselves. While Porter describes a process spanning the last two hundred years, the ambiguous connection between democratization and quantification clearly echoes through the rhetoric of Big Data with renewed vigour and connects tightly to the intensifying "legitimation crisis" (Habermas 1973) traditional institutions and modes of authority have been experiencing.

Taken together, these elements explain why Big Data is perceived as technically and practically feasible, economically appealing, and socially – and even ethically – desirable.

Data Analysis and Accounting Realism

The turn to the empirical relies heavily on the proliferation of instances of data collection, but the ways these data are being made to signify is particularly relevant for understanding how normativity comes into play. To this end, the algorithms involved in analysis and automated decision making – which generally manifests as some kind of *ordering* (e.g. a ranked list, a categorization, etc.) – need to be distinguished into two morphological lines.

In the first case, the decision model is explicitly designed. The (in)famous impact factor for scientific journals, for example, is the average number of citations papers in a journal received in the two previous years. *Somebody*, in this case Eugene Garfield, decided that this would be a good formula to capture "impact" and a sufficient number of people agreed, turning the metric into a widely accepted means for ranking scientific publications. Outcomes can be – and are – presented as distributed decisions where every researcher gets her "vote", simply by citing others, but the calculative procedure has an identifiable author and, more importantly, a clear and stable content that can be scrutinized and criticized.

In the second case, however, the decision model is derived through statistical learning. A spam filter, for example, requires specimen of *spam* and *ham* emails from its users. Parsing through these examples, it will generate a decision model where each word becomes a probabilistic indicator for the two categories. If the word "Viagra" always appears in emails marked as spam and never as ham, it will become a strong indicator for "spamminess". All words are taken into account and if the combined score exceeds a certain level, the email is flagged as spam. This is, in a nutshell, how machine learning works and it removes the decision model a step further since it becomes *adaptive* (the classifier changes with shifting email content) and potentially *personalized* (my filter classifies differently from yours because my spam is your ham). There is still a calculative procedure, but it no longer contains a clear normative proposition like the Impact Factor; rather, it orchestrates how the empirical examples – the mails marked as spam or ham – are turned into a decision model through human feedback. Both the content and the author of the decision model become substantially vague (cf. Burrell 2016).

The second group of algorithms informs what I have called "interested readings of reality" (Rieder 2016), assessments that are not just applied in operational settings, but fully permeated by operational goals in terms of their epistemological makeup. We are currently witnessing the proliferation of a particular use of statistical techniques, which, in Desrosières' (2001) terms, does not subscribe to "metrological realism" predicated on a correspondence theory of truth, but to "accounting realism", an epistemological stance that assesses truth – or rather validity – in relation to an operational objective, for example profit maximization. Machine learning techniques fit the requirements of accounting realism almost perfectly since they are *inductive* in the sense that they do not test or apply a hypothesis (e. g. what spam looks like), but generate it from an *interested* appraisal of past experience. Most people are not keen on describing or theorizing spam, they simply want it gone. One could argue that the trained statistical classifier containing the probability values for all parsed words represents a "theory" of spam, but this theory will vary between users and, most importantly, is derived from feedback rather than explicitly laid out.

This has profound consequences for how decisions come to be made and how judgement is operationalized. Rather than formulating a theory of what makes a "good" employee, which may be seen as tainted by common biases, a manager may turn to machine learning for counsel on hiring by submitting a set of well-structured CVs of excellent current or past employees to the computer. The learning technique will then derive ("learn") a statistical model consisting of correlations between the CV data and the performance assessment as target variable – the component carrying what I call *interest*[5]. In the case of spam, it is the binary value spam/ham that is trained for, while in a hiring process it may be the number of sales or some other stand-in for "good performance". The statistical

---

5   It is important to note that this need not be monetary value. The manager may very well decide that she is looking for the funniest hire possible and select the employee CVs used for training according to their capacity to entertain the office. The classifier will then correlate the submitted data with that assessment and produce a decision model. But, as Desrosières (2001: 342) argues, accounting realism generally relies on *money* as general equivalent.

model can then be used to classify incoming job candidates according to their predicted performance. This requires relatively little discretion or judgment from the manager other than the trust in the method itself, since using job performance as target variable would hardly seem controversial. If the CVs used to train the model happen to indicate that employees with higher educational attainment generate higher value for the company, the model will reflect that. Just like the spam filter, every variable present in the CVs will be correlated with the desired outcome.

Readers concerned with metrological truth may protest that correlation does not mean causation. They may interject that there is no "raw" data (cf. Gitelman 2013; van Dijck 2014), that the data used in machine learning is itself *produced* in various ways – skewed, incomplete, and generated through interfaces that more often than not impose discrete choices on fluid matters. They may, more fundamentally, take issue with the very idea that often highly decontextualized data can be used to produce adequate knowledge about complex social situations that require a "situated and embodied" (Haraway 1988) perspective. These objections would clearly have merit – and yet miss the point. The epistemological problem of accounting realism is not to *describe* the sociological makeup of society, but to *decide* whether a given job candidate should be hired or not. The goal is not truthful description, but good – i.e. profitable – decision-making in situations where too much information meets too little time. What matters most, here, is that contemporary forms of mechanical reasoning propose methods that seemingly circumvent normative commitment by turning to the empirical, reading it through the lens of operational goals. Judgement, understood as the evaluation of evidence to make a decision, becomes a product of statistical analysis and thus acquires an aura of objectivity, rationality, and – most importantly – a legitimacy that derives from its empirical underpinnings. The manager in our CV example could easily claim that her decision was as objective as they come. Not only on account of the computational technique used, but also because productivity in monetary terms is the very value or interest seen as requiring no further justification. So where is the problem? To answer this question, we first need to make a detour to comment on the makeup of contemporary societies, which constitute the material data analysis processes.

Structured Societies and Big Data

Data proliferate in contemporary societies because an ever growing number of things we do are, in one way or another, touched by computerization. Mediation through interfaces, databases, and algorithms may well involve a loss of immediacy or some other element of "artificialization", but this can be said of all aspects of culture. For all intents and purposes, the technical environments we inhabit are, indeed, our *real*, and the data these environments produce so effortlessly reflect part of it. There would be many caveats to add at this point, but for the sake of the argument I am trying to develop, I propose that we consider the possibility that the masses of data are not a hallucinatory fever dream, but a somewhat spotty and skewed window on societies that are, in part, organized through the same technical structures that produce these data in the first place. Their analysis therefore reveals our societies, at least particular aspects from particular vantage points. When reflecting on potential ramifications of Big Data and the machine learning techniques I just described, we need to think about what it means to know these societies through the lens of accounting realism.

Modernity, and in particular the period since the Second World War, is characterized by processes of *individualization* and *diversification* of situations and styles of living (Beck 1986: 122). The emergence of consumer capitalism has shifted the focus from production to consumption and produces an ever more fine-grained variety of products and experiences in virtually all areas of human existence, from food to cultural goods and vacations. Societies adopting liberal democracy have seen many traditional social segmentations and taboos erode, continuously extending individuals' capacities to live lives that differ substantially from those lived by both previous generations and the next door neighbours. According to Giddens, ours are decentred, non-traditional societies "where social bonds have effectively to be *made,* rather than inherited from the past" (1994: 107) and where "choice has become obligatory" (1994: 76). One may rightfully wonder whether there is any "real" difference between the many breakfast cereals available in every supermarket, but my objective, here, is not to adjudicate whether these variations in patterns of consumption, in socio-economic status, in geographical anchoring, in political and social values, in sexual preferences, in cultural identities and tastes, and so forth are meaningful or not. The argument I want to put forward is threefold: first, we live in societies characterized by high degrees of diversity in terms of lived lives; second, these lives are constantly logged and surveyed in various ways, leading to enormous amounts of data that reflect (some of) their diverse character; third, these lived lives are *patterned* and not random. The last point requires additional elaboration.

The social sciences have spent the last two-hundred years trying to understand how individuals and society relate, how variation and commonality entwine to produce complex and dynamic arrangements that stabilize through various continuities and institutions. The most common term used to address stability in society is that of *structure,* whether it is understood descriptively to denote non-randomness or analytically to refer to actual social forces. The notion of social structure is partially tied to instances of group membership, both externally attributed or used by actors to demarcate themselves. Categories along the lines of estate, class, caste, ethnicity, race, nationality, profession, and so forth are the result of historically produced (socioeconomic) classification and stratification that resulted in more or less consistent groups that shared characteristics and social standing, which, in turn, differentiated them from other groups. These segmentations have – at least in part – lost their "binding force" (Giddens 1994: 63) and structuring capacity, as well as their utility as descriptive concepts. Traditional arrangements have been disrupted and the new ones are more complex, dynamic, and opaque.

One may wonder in how far attempts to think social structure from the bottom up are reactions to these transformations. Simmel's (1908) "social geometry" can already be seen as a way of conceptualizing "societification" *(Vergesellschaftung)* from the individual, who, due to increasing social differentiation, enters into complex relationships with various others and is less and less confined to her primary group. The recent interest in Tarde's monadological understanding of society (Latour et al. 2012), as well as the continued popularity of other "atomistic" currents – from social exchange theory to social network analysis – can be seen as methodological trends or, more fundamentally, as attempts to grapple, conceptually, with decentred societies that are grouping in more flexible, transient, and diverse ways. However, if it has become hard to speak of a working class today, it is not because economic exploitation has disappeared, but because forms of economic exploitation have become too intricate and varied to summarize them easily into a clear-cut sociological concept. The diversity of lived lives does not imply equality and both domination and stratification continue to exist, even if their consequences are increasingly individualized.

But why am I talking about the shape of society and our conceptual means to describe it in a paper on Big Data? Because in a situation characterized by social differentiation on the one side and ambivalent forms of global and local integration on the other, data collection and analysis promise to make the social *legible* again, to reinstall mastery over societies that continuously diversify, creating differentiations that no longer conform to traditional groupings and categorizations. This is the *raison d'être* of computational data analysis. As complexity and opacity grow, the epistemic and commercial value of techniques that promise to produce viable descriptions and decisions grows as well. This promise, however, still hinges on the "structuredness" of society in the sense that elements may be arranged in increasingly complicated ways, yet not devolve into randomness. Forms of coherence, commonality, and stability continue to exist even if they can no longer be reduced to conceptual pivots such as class. As Giddens remarks, individuals' capacity to make decisions in virtually every sphere of life does not guarantee egalitarian pluralism since "it is also a medium of power and of stratification" (1994: 76). And Bourdieu's (1979) assessment that different forms of capital – economic, social, and cultural – are connected in various ways still holds as well, which means that, for example, years of education, level of income, and cultural tastes correlate. Forms of analysis that make it possible to analyse and act upon such multivariate relationships spanning different domains of life proliferate for this very reason. A recent study in attribute prediction makes a good case in point:

"Facebook Likes can be used to automatically and accurately predict a range of highly sensitive personal attributes including: sexual orientation, ethnicity, religious and political views, personality traits, intelligence, happiness, use of addictive substances, parental separation, age, and gender." (Kosinski et al. 2013: 5802)

One may rightfully interject that the researchers used contestable concepts, for example concerning gender, but this would, again, apply criticism from the epistemological headspace of metrological realism to procedures that are more deliberately applied in settings where accounting realism dominates. To put it bluntly: in a situation where the task is to distinguish between a seemingly amorphous mass of customers or other entities, the benchmark is not necessarily to get the prediction right in every case, but to make (quick) decisions *that are more accurate than a coin toss*,[6] speculative inferences that produce an advantageous outcome more often than not. And machine learning generally performs much better than that. The above mentioned study, for example, was able to predict gender with an accuracy of 0.93 and sexual orientation with 0.88. In many cases, a level of 0.51 would be enough to justify applying the technique. The targeting of advertisement, for example, does not have to be perfect to make it economically attractive, merely better than purely random placement. Machine learning is a powerful way to produce such better-than-coin-toss performance at very little cost and it has the additional benefit of providing an empiricist narrative that includes a widely acceptable rationale as well as moments of testability and verifiability when effects, for example on click-through rates, can be directly observed.

Publications like *Dataclysm* by Christian Rudder (2010), one of the co-founders of the dating site OkCupid, provide many examples for patterns and correlations between gender, race, class, and cultural tastes that may seem spurious until one considers their considerable commercial potential. Data mining reveals these structures and social fault lines, and it can order individual cases or ad-hoc groups accordingly. The connection with potential social and political ramifications becomes clear when one considers that, first, decisions based on data analysis can have concrete consequences and, second, the existing structures in society, seen through the lens of data, are informing these decisions. A recent paper on data mining's "disparate impact" formulates the issue clearly:

"Data mining takes the existing state of the world as a given, and ranks candidates according to their predicted attributes in *that* world." (Barocas/Selbst 2016: 731)

That world, *our* world, is ripe with inequalities and the large and small variations between (datafied) individuals are becoming easily detectable and practical to

---

[6] There are, of course, many areas where higher precision is required, but this (slight) exaggeration should again highlight the fundamental difference between metrological and accounting realism in terms of their epistemic requirements.

distinguish and sort. The structures of differentiation are *read* from an interested perspective and the interest is, more often than not, tied to performance targets: lower loan default ratios, more productive employees, longer time on site, higher click-through rates, and so forth. Big Data, then, is a means to know and act on society on the basis of an empiricism that is epistemically biased in a way that the opposition between objective and subjective does not capture: it is, in a sense, a most impartial way to pursue deeply partial objectives. The capacity to make every data point signify in relation to a goal is the starting point of the third part of my argument, which is concerned with its social and political significance.

Data Mining and the Question of Values

A return to recent developments in sociological theory and methodology can help us gain a better understanding of how data mining produces both interested readings of the data it processes and specific "levers on 'reality'"[7] that reach back into society. The question of social grouping is, again, crucial. Musing on the new availability of datasets and analytical tools, Bruno Latour and colleagues have recently argued that the differentiation between micro and macro, between individuals and aggregates is gradually rendered obsolete as it becomes "possible to account for longer lasting features of social order by learning to navigate through overlapping 'monads' instead of alternating between the two levels of individual and aggregate" (2012: 592). But as researchers navigate digital data not by moving "from the particular to the general, but from particular to more particulars" (2012: 599), aggregating and individualizing at will, so do the algorithmic tools used in settings ruled by accounting realism. The notion of the group ceases to be a stable analytical category and becomes a speculative ensemble assembled to inform a decision and to enable a course of action. The *creditworthy*, for example, are not a distinct class of people, but those the decision model deems capable, at this instant, to pay back a loan – and nothing more. Ordered for a different purpose, the groups scatter and reassemble differently. Foucault (1976: 183) still felt the need to distinguish between *anatomo-politics* targeting the individual and *bio-politics* aiming at the population, even if he contended that they are necessarily linked. When considering contemporary data analysis, this distinction melts before our eyes. We witness the emergence of methods that define units and ensembles at will and project the individual as element of ad-hoc aggregates and vice versa. All of this means that fine-grained differentiation between people, things, or situations – a task which used to be difficult and costly – is becoming easy and cheap,

---

7   Goody argues that writing facilitates information ordering and retrieval through decontextualization and thereby "gives the mind a special kind of lever on 'reality'" (1977: 109).

making it feasible to individualize and aggregate far beyond the granularity of postal codes, income brackets, gender, or skin colour.

Does this mean that data mining will usher in a future without discriminations based on race or gender? If the rhetoric of impartiality and fairness that accompanies data-driven decision-making is an indication, we should not dismiss the possibility outright. But caveats apply. Recent work on data mining (Calders/Verwer 2010; Custers et al. 2013) have put the finger on how even in highly diversified societies seemingly "innocent" variables, such as cultural tastes, correlate strongly with class, gender, race, and so forth, making it easy to dissimulate explicitly discriminatory decisions, even if the race of a person is not directly assessable. Moreover, insufficient or erroneous data may lead to effects of statistical discrimination if certain groups are over- or underrepresented. But there is a set of more complicated issues that point to the core of the normative argument I am trying to make. The notion of "objective racism" (Barocas/Selbst 2016) highlights the troubling fact that race and other "sensitive attributes" correlate with variables that would seem uncontroversial, for example educational achievement as a factor in hiring decisions. The problem, here, is not that data mining can be biased, but that, after centuries of inequality and discrimination, *empirical reality is biased*. This problem has led to proposals that operate on principles similar to affirmative action (Calders/Verwer 2010). But these solutions require the sensitive attribute to be explicitly present in the data in order to correct for it, which may not be feasible in certain contexts, and they indeed raise the question which attributes should be singled out in the first place. It is in this sense that the very makeup of contemporary societies again comes into view.

Even if one could find ways to create somewhat equal starting conditions, a society that attempts to produce *fair* competition by correcting for past discrimination is by no means one that eschews picking winners and losers. Behind the question of how Big Data may disadvantage particular groups sits the broader issue of what it means for a society that fully embraces many forms of competition and discrimination if every data trace can be used to decide "who should be targeted for special treatment, suspicion, eligibility, inclusion, access, and so on" (Lyon 2003: 20). In contemporary western societies, the ideal of *meritocracy* provides a widely shared normative horizon that justifies instances of selection, hierarchisation, and, indeed, disparate impact, even if – or precisely because – it is considered to be at least partially responsible for the breaking up of segmentations based on gender, ethnicity, and race (Kett 2012). Traditionally, meritocracy installs (educational) achievement as selection mechanism and relies on credentials and tests to signal these achievements. Data driven assessments allow for the inclusion of a much wider array of factors and for the extension of the principle to new applications such as the modulation of health insurance payments based on individuals' level of physical activity. This supports the larger trend towards a setting where "[m]eritocracy has shifted from impersonal technology to a situation where the relation between abilities and rewards has been deeply personalised" (Allen

2012: 5). The use of data analysis for hiring decisions is one specific case, but the proliferation of Big Data implies that many other sorting decisions can and will be made on broad assessments of individuals' seemingly superfluous data traces, which can nevertheless become meaningful and actionable indicators when considered as part of the webs of correlation that permeate structured societies. Due to incomplete or faulty data and errors in speculative prediction, but also due to the fact that the ponderation of the factors going into a decision are both fundamentally opaque (Burrell 2016) and potentially dynamic, people may find themselves in conditions of *paranoid meritocracy*, constantly wondering whether their practices and preferences signal their adherence to "economic morality" (Allen 2012) and their genuine desire to contribute and succeed.

One way to think about possible outcomes are generalized versions of the credit score mechanism, which records individuals' financial behaviour and computes a score that is supposed to express their creditworthiness. Explicit attempts in that direction, such as China's "social credit" score[8], can be understood as disciplinary mechanisms, but they also call attention to the question of social values that is made explicit in such endeavours. While scholars rightfully criticize Big Data and associated practices in terms of method, we should not forget that data mining implements deeply value-laden perspectives due to the normativity implied in the target variable. As I have already mentioned, the legitimacy of data-driven decision-making hinges not only on the presumed objectivity of its methods, but on the unquestioned acceptance of productivity, performance, merit, and, in short, of "economic morality [as a] guiding logic that conditions and directs our daily lives" (Allen 2012: 19).

In extremis, Big Data may simply be a means to project our current value systems more pervasively, thoroughly, and effectively into society. This would then mean that a critique of Big Data requires a critique of these values, for example of meritocracy. As Dahrendorf remarks, "nowadays meritocracy seems to be simply another version of the inequality that characterises all societies" and it may even be "a particularly cruel form of inequality, as those who do not succeed cannot argue that they were unlucky or kept down by those in power" (2005). While Kett (2012) notes that the ideal of merit was long perceived as a value in tension with equality, Littler argues that is has since become "an alibi for plutocracy" by "seizing the idea, practice and discourse of greater social equality" (2013: 69).

Seen through this lens, Big Data appears as a means to extend the logic of pervasive and skewed competition, paired with the rhetoric of impartiality, into further spheres of life. The idea that Big Data "works" – in the scope set by accounting realism – may, then, be much more terrifying than its possible failure. What if the real problem is not too little, but too much objectivity? What if the problem is knowing individuals and groups too well rather than not well enough? What if our Facebook Likes are, indeed, indicative of our future job performance? What if

---

8 "China 'social credit': Beijing sets up huge system", 26 October, 2015 (http://www.bbc.com/news/world-asia-china-34592186).

the saying "ignorance is bliss" holds true for society more generally, in the sense that *not-knowing* creates spaces where a plurality of practices and lives is possible because we cannot mechanically relate them to notions of performance and profit?

Conclusions

In concluding the somewhat experimental argument developed in this paper, I want to posit that the grand challenge of universally available data is not only surveillance understood as permanent policing, but also surveillance understood as permanent appraisal of compatibility with economic morality, the dominant value in contemporary society. It is certainly not new that differentiation, in all its forms, implies economic opportunity. But acting on the networks of difference that characterize our societies used to be costly. In many cases, it no longer is and, as a consequence, the many inequalities that persist in our societies are quickly becoming more consequential. Data mining and associated techniques have begun to read these inequalities from the perspective of operational goals. We would be well advised, however, to scrutinize not only the methods, but also the goals and the values that inform them.

The story of Rolf Buchholz, the current record holder in number of body piercings, makes for an instructive parable for the paradox of diversity. While Buchholz was denied entry into Dubai because airport staff feared he may practice black magic[9], he works apparently without any issues as a computer engineer with Deutsche Telekom in Germany. As long as he complies with the tenets of economic morality, the way he decorates his body is simply irrelevant. This is how contemporary capitalism liberates. But the moment Buchholz' job performance dips, his job is up for grabs. This is how contemporary capitalism disciplines. Even if the principle is not fully implemented, the direction is clear: diversity is welcome, as long as it does not interfere with the bottom line. In practice, however, there is one other thing keeping Buchholz from losing his job, namely Germany's labour laws. These laws are an example for deliberate limits to generalized economic morality and Big Data will increasingly force us to consider such limits.

As interested reading of reality, data mining makes it possible to assess economic utility in profound ways. In order to tame accounting realism, we therefore need to engage these techniques as deep, embedded, and performative forms of judgment, as modes of governing through measuring. Critique should strive to combine two different pathways. The first concerns the problems, limitations, and biases of the method. Here, Big Data's claims need to be critically examined. But the second needs to take these claims at face value and ask how the growing capacity to know society highlights the deep ambiguities in the dominant value system.

9 "World's most pierced man Rolf Buchholz barred from Dubai", August 17, 2014 (http://www.bbc.com/news/world-middle-east-28831106).

References

Allen, Ansgar (2012): "Life Without the 'X' Factor: Meritocracy Past and Present." In: Power and Education 4/1, pp. 4–19.
Andrejevic, Mark (2013): Infoglut, New York-Abingdon: Routledge.
Barocas, Solon/Selbst, Andrew D. (2016): "Big Data's Disparate Impact." In: California Law Review 104/3, pp. 671–732.
Beck, Ulrich (1986): Risikogesellschaft, Frankfurt am Main: Suhrkamp.
Boltanski, Luc/Chiapello, Ève (1999): Le nouvel esprit du capitalisme, Paris: Gallimard.
Burrell, Jenna (2016): "How the Machine 'Thinks': Understanding Opacity in Machine Learning Algorithms." In: Big Data & Society 3/1.
Bourdieu, Pierre (1979): La distinction, Paris: Editions de Minuit.
Calders, Toon/Verwer, Sicco (2010): "Three naive Bayes approaches for discrimination-free classification." In: Data Mining and Knowledge Discovery 21/2, pp. 277–292.
Custers, Bart/Calders, Toon/Schermer, Bart/Zarsky, Tal (2013): Discrimination and Privacy in the Information Society, Berlin-Heidelberg: Springer.
Dahrendorf, Ralf (2005): "The Rise and Fall of Meritocracy." In: Project Syndicate, April 13 (https://www.project-syndicate.org/commentary/the-rise-and-fall-of-meritocracy).
Ekbia, Hamid et al. (2015): "Big Data, Bigger Dilemmas: A Critical Review." In: Journal of the Association for Information Science and Technology Volume 66/8, pp. 1523–1545.
Executive Office of the President of the United States, "Big Data and Differential Pricing", February 2015 (https://www.whitehouse.gov/sites/default/files/docs/Big_Data_Report_Nonembargo_v2.pdf).
Foucault, Michel (1976): Histoire de la sexualité 1. La volonté de savoir, Paris: Gallimard.
Giddens, Anthony (1994): "Living in a Post-Traditional Society." In: Ulrich Beck/Anthony Giddens/Scott Lash (eds.): Reflexive Modernization Politics. Tradition and Aesthetics in the Modern Social Order, Stanford: Stanford University Press, pp. 56–109.
Gitelman, Lisa (2013): "Raw Data" Is an Oxymoron, Cambridge, MA: MIT Press.
Goody, Jack (1977): The Domestication of the Savage Mind, Cambridge, UK: Cambridge University Press.
Haraway, Donna (1988): "Situated Knowledges: The Science Question in Feminism and the Privilege of Partial Perspective." In: Feminist Studies 14/3, pp. 575–599.
Hume, David (1739): A Treatise of Human Nature, London: John Noon.
Kett, Joseph F. (2012): Merit: The History of a Founding Ideal, Ithaca: Cornell University Press.

Kitchin, Rob (2014): "Big Data, New Epistemologies and Paradigm Shifts." In: Big Data & Society 1/1.

Kitchin, Rob (2016): "Thinking Critically About and Researching Algorithms." In: Information, Communication & Society 19/1, pp. 14–29.

Kosinski, Michal/Stillwell, David/Graepel, Thore (2013): "Private Traits and Attributes Are Predictable from Digital Records of Human Behavior." In: PNAS 110/15, pp. 5802–5805.

Latour, Bruno/Jensen, Pablo/Venturini, Tommaso/Grauwin, Sébastian/Boullier, Dominique (2012): "'The Whole is Always Smaller than its Parts' – a Digital Test of Gabriel Tardes' Monads." In: The British Journal of Sociology 63/4, pp. 590–615.

Littler, Jo (2013): "Meritocracy as Plutocracy: the Marketising of 'Equality' Under Neoliberalism." In: New Formations 80-81, pp. 52–72.

Lyon, David (2003): Surveillance as Social Sorting, London-New York: Routledge.

Porter, Theodore M. (1995): Trust in Numbers, Princeton: Princeton University Press.

Rieder, Bernhard (2016): "Scrutinizing an Algorithmic Technique: The Bayes Classifier as Interested Reading of Reality." Information, Communication & Society, 19/1, pp. 100–117.

Rudder, Christian (2014): Dataclysm, New York: Crown.

Simmel, Georg (1908): Soziologie, Berlin: Duncker & Humblot.

Sweeney, Latanya (2013): "Discrimination in Online Ad Delivery." In: Communications of the Association of Computing Machinery 56/5, pp. 44–54.

van Dijck, José (2014): "Datafication, Dataism and Dataveillance: Big Data Between Scientific Paradigm and Ideology." In: Surveillance & Society 12/2, pp. 197–208.

Digital Epistemologies

The Alternative Epistemologies of Data Activism

Stefania Milan, Lonneke van der Velden

Abstract

As datafication progressively invades all spheres of contemporary society, citizens grow increasingly aware of the critical role of information as the new fabric of social life. This awareness triggers new forms of civic engagement and political action that we term "data activism". Data activism indicates the range of sociotechnical practices that interrogate the fundamental paradigm shift brought about by datafication. Combining Science and Technology Studies with Social Movement Studies, this theoretical article offers a foretaste of a research agenda on data activism. It foregrounds democratic agency vis-à-vis datafication, and unites under the same label ways of affirmative engagement with data ("proactive data activism", e.g. data-based advocacy) and tactics of resistance to massive data collection ("reactive data activism", e.g. encryption practices), understood as a continuum along which activists position and reposition themselves and their tactics. The article argues that data activism supports the emergence of novel epistemic cultures within the realm of civil society, making sense of data as a way of knowing the world and turning it into a point of intervention and generation of data countercultures. It offers the notion of data activism as a heuristic tool for the study of new forms of political participation and civil engagement in the age of datafication, and explores data activism as an evolving theoretical construct susceptible to contestation and revision.

Keywords: datafication; data activism; democratic agency; Big Data epistemologies; Social Movement Studies; Science and Technology Studies.

Acknowledgements

This article was researched with the support of a Starting Grant of the European Research Council, awarded to Stefania Milan as Principal Investigator (ERC_StG-2014_639379; https://data-activism.net). The authors wish to thank the editors of this special issue; the anonymous reviewers; Prof. Sandra Braman

(Texas A&M); the attendees to the *Contentious Data* workshop (Amsterdam, 15–16 September 2016); the participants to the data activism sessions at the 2016 conferences of the International Communication Association (Fukuoka, 10 June) and of the Association of Internet Researchers (Berlin, 7 October) for the invaluable critical questions and insights. Our gratitude extends also to the DATACTIVE team at the University of Amsterdam for the inspiring conversations.

Introduction

It was the summer of 2012 when the Italian hacker and artist Salvatore Iaconesi was diagnosed with brain cancer. Still hospitalised, he "hacked" his medical data to make them accessible to non-experts, published them online, and launched *La Cura*, a "participatory performance aimed at redefining the word 'cure', bringing it out of hospitals [...] back into society" (Iaconesi 2016). He invited anyone in the world to send him a cure. Over half a million people contributed advice and emotional support.

In 2012, British unemployed finance worker Eliot Higgins, also known as Brown Moses, turned into a weapon analyst by systematically monitoring videos of the Syrian conflict on YouTube, experimenting with a new form of "social media weapon tracking". In 2014, he founded Bellingcat.com, a platform for self-taught open-source intelligence (OSINT) analysts and investigative journalists, which gained the praise of Amnesty International, among others (O'Brien 2013).

In order to support citizen witnessing and improving grassroots documentation efforts, the Guardian Project has developed the mobile application CameraV. It captures and archives image metadata as an extra layer of contextual verification, making possible the potential use of the footage as evidential proof in court. The footage is password-protected, encrypted and stored on the user's device (The Guardian Project: n.d.).

With the progressive datafication of an ever-expanding range of human activities – from personal health to interpersonal connections, from public administration to security – people become increasingly aware of the critical role of information in contemporary societies. The anecdotes opening this article belong to the realm of the transformative experiments that see citizens putting data to new uses, developing "new rationalities and alternative social imaginaries around datafication" (Baack 2015: 8). These "moments where meaningful change can occur, even if those changes are [...] tinged with technocracy" (Schrock 2016: 583), speak to the unprecedented possibility for larger publics to foster social change by engaging in data politics. But today's massive data collection is also employed for monitoring people, as we know from the classified information leaked by whistleblower Edward Snowden (Lyon 2015). Users' online activities are regularly "sucked up as data, quantified and classified, making possible real-time tracking and monitoring" (Lyon 2014: 4), which generates an unparalleled power asymmetry between the state and its citizens (Brunton/Nissenbaum 2015). What for some observers is the hopeful "industrial revolution of data" (Hellerstein 2008), represents a new form of "surveillance capitalism" for others (Zuboff 2015).

While the industry as well as the state apparatus have long acknowledged the value of massive data collection for their activities, the so-called civil society – the realm of human activity outside the state and the market – is now slowly but steadily catching up and turning "big data" to its own ends. Civic hackers "requesting, digesting, contributing, modelling and contesting data" (Schrock 2016: 584) and civic tech activists (Russon Gilman 2016) seek to improve institutional output and democratic governance by means of software and data. Tech-savvy people experiment with arguably "radical" (Birchall 2014) transparency devices for the analysis of previously closed or hidden data (Heemsbergen 2014). In the footsteps of WikiLeaks, a range of whistle-blower platforms such as GlobalLeaks and PubLeaks has emerged, allowing for the tech-mediated protected transfer of data to journalists and/or the citizenry at large. Activists engage in "information activism" by monitoring powerful actors and curating datasets (Ganesh/Hankey 2015). Data visualisation is entering the activists' skillset; capacity building projects and knowledge sharing manuals increasingly target low-skill users (Tactical Tech Collective 2013; 2016). Activists become progressively aware of how the use of digital tools plays out technically, politically, and economically, rethinking what the "politics of data" means for their own practice, especially in the context of surveillance (Ganesh/Hankey 2015). They increasingly seek to counter massive data collection by means of resistance and obfuscation. Although the circumvention of surveillance is a long-standing practice amongst social movements and certainly predates datafication (see, e.g., della Porta 1995), dedicated events, trainings, and off-the-shelves tools to secure digital communications have mushroomed over the last few years (Aouragh et al. 2015), and encryption features prominently in counter-surveillance initiatives (Gürses/Kundnani/van Hoboken 2016). We subsume these diverse manifestations of an emerging "critical" attitude towards datafication under the rubric of "data activism".

This theoretical article explores the notion of data activism as a heuristic, polysemic tool to think politically about big data from the perspective of users and citizens, analysing in particular the contemporary evolution of activism vis-à-vis datafication. In what follows, we offer a conceptual map to approach grassroots engagement with data by combining insights from Social Movement Studies (SMS) and Science and Technology Studies (STS). First, we situate the notion of data activism in the domain of digital activism. Second, we show that data activism practices point to the emergence of novel epistemic cultures arising from within the civil society realm. Third, we explore the potential of data activism as a heuristic tool for empirical analysis and theoretical development. Finally, we sketch a future research agenda on data activism. In so doing, we intend to contribute to the study of "the variable ways in which power and participation are constructed and enacted" (Couldry/Powell 2014: 1) in bottom up data practices.

Defining data activism

Big data evokes a broad set of socio-technical phenomena enveloped in quasi-mythological narratives that univocally emphasise possibility and magnitude. Kitchin, however, showed that big data goes well beyond a matter of data volume, and "is characterised by being generated continuously, seeking to be exhaustive and fine-grained in scope, and flexible and scalable in its production" (2014: 2). For the purposes of our analysis, which underscores human agency in relation to data and technology, we understand big data as information-related tasks whose complexity requires individuals to take action with the support of software (cf. Cukier/Mayer-Schoenberger 2013). We take big data to refer also to "human subjects data, since it mainly (though not universally) consists of data about, and produced by, people" (Dalton/Taylor/Thatcher 2016: 2). While deliberately glossing over the nature of the data in question, these definitions stress the transformative and empowering potential of (any) data, focusing on the complexity of the tasks that can be performed rather than data magnitude, and on the socio-cultural meaning of said tasks. We consider data as a technology in itself, looking back to the semantic roots of the latter: the ancient Greek noun *techne*, "making", referred to what both art and engineering have in common (Braman 2004: 4). Seeing data as a technology allows us to call attention to what people do and can do with it.

The notion of data activism is not entirely new. Earlier characterisations have focused on particular instances of data-driven contestation, emphasizing aspects as different as the affective potential of the engagement with data, the contribution to institutional reform, and the relation with governance. For instance, Renzi and Langlois explored how data partake in generating individual and collective action, which they describe as "new modes of being and acting together through a direct engagement with data and the means of its mobilisation" (2015: 203). Their notion of data activism highlights how alternative media are re-appropriations but also sites for experimentation that allow for the generation of new affective bonds. Focusing instead on the relation between the state and its citizens, Schrock coined the heading of "data activism and advocacy" to identify contemporary civic hackers who "operate through a range of data-driven political modes [...] to bring about systemic change [...] [and] participate in civic data politics" (2016: 591), with the aim to ameliorate the governance process and output.

To be sure, data activism comes close to other variations of the wide-ranging category of cyber- or digital activism (McCaughey/Ayers 2003), such as hacktivism (Jordan/Taylor 2004), statactivism (Bruno/Didier/Prévieux 2014), and information politics (Jordan 2015). Hacktivism indicates "collective action in cyberspace that addresses network infrastructure or exploits the infrastructure's technical and ontological features for political or social change" (Milan 2015a: 550). Similarly, data activists might engage with the infrastructure of platforms and code. They, too, "engage in politically motivated use of technical expertise in view of fixing society through software and online action" (ibid.). Yet, our notion of data activism outgrows the engagement with infrastructure to embrace information and knowledge as a broader category of intervention.

Looking at the prescriptive potential of numbers, Bruno and colleagues coined the notion of statactivism, a portmanteau of statistics and activism identifying the bottom-up experiments aimed at the re-appropriation of statistics' power of denunciation and emancipation (Bruno/Didier/Prévieux 2014). The role of statistics in statactivism is two-fold: to criticise reality and to represent it, mobilizing "numbers, measurements and indicators as means of denunciation and criticism" (Bruno/Didier/Vitale 2014: 199). Similar to data activists, statactivists operate simultaneously inside and outside institutions, and numbers are a means of both disclosure and affirmation (ibid.). However, data activism as a theoretical category embraces a broader range of encounters with datafication: on the one hand, it comprises but also exceeds numbers as source of truth claims, and on the other, it understands datafication as conveying risks as well. Consequently, data activism bears the promise to incorporate a wider set of tactical responses.

Finally, Jordan's expansive notion of information politics (2015) engages with the contentious reactions to mass digital cultures along with network and control protocols, pointing to antagonistic formations in which information politics becomes part of conflicts over exploitation and liberation. While our notion of data activism presupposes the possibility for contention and rebellion, we understand data activism as a series of nuanced phenomena that position themselves in a continuum between contestation and recognition. In this vein, we offer the notion of data activism as yet another possible manifestation of activism in the information society – one that, however, explicitly engages with the new forms information and knowledge and their production take today, challenging dominant understandings of datafication. As such, thinking in terms of data activism has something to offer to the reflection on the ubiquity of digital communication and mediation dynamics in the platform society (e.g., Castells 2009; van Dijck 2013), as well as on the nature of contemporary activism and its evolving protest/media configurations (e.g., Bennett 2012; Bennett/Segerberg 2013; Milan 2015b).

The data activism rubric embraces the composite series of sociotechnical practices that, emerging at the fringes of the contemporary activism ecology, interrogate datafication and its socio-political consequences. We deliberately unite under the same label two variations of grassroots data politics – affirmative engagement with data and resistance to massive data collection – which are often considered contrasting with each other. Yet, they both address and interrogate the fundamental paradigm shift brought about by datafication.

Our notion of data activism foregrounds democratic agency vis-à-vis datafication. Two elements rest at its core: its sociotechnical nature and the mobilisation factor. First, following the path traced by STS, we emphasise the fundamental interaction between people, information, and technology that constitutes emerging formations of data activism. Data activism is deeply rooted in, and thus enabled and constrained by data and software, both its availability and its pursuit – and this special relation shapes tactics, identities, and modes of organizing. Second, from a SMS perspective data activism can be seen as an form of socio-political mobilisation, as it brings people (and information and technology) together for some kind of action variably contentious in nature, and explicitly addressing, confronting, or engaging with datafication. Mobilisation here embraces both discrete events – individual and collective acts of appropriation of data, but also of dissent, subversion, and resistance to data collection – and the overall process that subtends to the emergence of data activism – namely, the raising popular concern signaling a fundamental change in perspective and attitude towards datafication that is slowly emerging within civil society.

The social forces supporting these incipient activism practices are not new. Users have long appropriated and repurposed media technology for self-expression and social change, experimenting with up-and-coming media technology – be it phone, print, radio, fax, or the internet (see Marvin 1990; Downing 2011). The most tech-aware amongst radical openness activists have experimented with technical ways of circumventing state control since the 1980s – advocating, for example, for a crypto anarchy in communications which would be made possible by cryptography (May 1992). Emerging from the smoking ashes of their predecessors and variably intersecting other contemporary trends like citizen science (Irwin 1995) and sensing (Gabrys 2016), biohacking (Delfanti 2013), citizen data journalism (Gray/Chambers/Bounegru 2012), the quantified self (Lupton 2016) and the transparency movements (Sifry 2011), current data activism practices are largely modelled after hacker cultures and rituals (Levy 1984) and the do-it-yourself approach of makerspaces, hacklabs, and hackerspaces (Maxigas 2012). Similar to grassroots radio producers (Dunbar-Hester 2012), the radical techies of the 1990s (Milan 2013), and the open-source movement (Coleman 2013), data activists often preach technical engagement as a way of confronting elite expertise and taking control over the technology of daily use. From their forerunners, data activists have borrowed the hands-on attitude, and the notions of access to information, code tinkering, collaboration, and world improvement through technical fixes. And because datafication is such a prominent feature in public life, data activism, as a mode of dealing with it, might progressively appeal to more diverse communities of concerned citizens, beyond the expert niche of previous incarnations of tech activist engagement.

Data activism shapes novel epistemic cultures

Datafication alters "the conditions under which we can make sense of our world and our own actions", affecting "our capacity to act with agency" (Baack 2015: 1). Big data has far-reaching epistemological consequences, affecting "how knowledge is produced, business conducted, and governance enacted" (Kitchin 2014: 2). It "reframes key questions about the constitution of knowledge" (boyd/Crawford

2012: 665). Algorithms, too, have the "ability to shape perceived realities [...] not only by enabling certain representations of the world around us, but also by enticing us to internalise these realities and make them our own" (Renzi/Langlois 2015: 202). Further, big data and their representations tend to reify the future, crystallizing *a* reality – usually quantified, and presented as neutral and infallible – as the only possible one and narrowing down the options for alternatives (cf. Chun 2011). In other words, what is known as big data constitutes a novel, powerful system of knowledge with its own epistemology that is to say a specific way of framing, packaging, presenting and activating information and knowledge.

Framing, packaging and presenting data are productive exercises, which have the potential to alter not only our vision of the world, but also our own theory of knowledge, so to speak. The current emphasis on computational analysis and machine learning as core (and qualitatively superior) ways of understanding the social world, moulds the way people relate to information and knowledge. Furthermore, "big" data are often seductively staged, accompanied as they typically are by attractive visualisations and graphs that simplify reality and communicate it in immediate and efficient ways (see Cairo 2012). What is then the role of data activism in these dynamics? If data is not a given nor is it ever raw (Gitelman 2013), data activism can be seen as an exercise in creating alternative ways of seeing the world, while opening up questions about the positivism ethos of the so-called "data revolution".

Fraser (2005) criticised the state-centric "politics of representation", identifying in the control by the elites over the framing of political representation a form of injustice. "Making discourses", on the contrary, entails "producing new languages or modifying old ones so as to find words for novel phenomena" (Jasanoff 2004: 39–41). We argue that data activism practices signal that new epistemic cultures are emerging within the civil society realm: a way (or, better, ways) of making counter-discourses and data countercultures that challenge the mainstream readings of reality.

Epistemic cultures shape the way we relate to knowledge and its validation, how we understand and filter the world around us as well as our experiences. They represent "cultures of creating and warranting knowledge" (Knorr Cetina/Reichmann 2015: 873). When the notion was introduced in laboratory studies in the late 1990s, it disrupted the idea of "epistemic unity" of the sciences, by stressing diversity in modes of knowledge making (ibid.). This concept invites us to look at the "specific strategies that generate, validate, and communicate scientific accomplishments", and to take into account the complex "relationships between experts, organisational formats, and epistemic objects" (873–4). The emerging epistemic cultures propelled by data activism point to innovative and potentially transformative ways of relating to big data and its consequences.

Postulating a critical/active engagement with data, its forms, dynamics, and infrastructure, data activists function as producers of counter-expertise and alternative epistemologies, making sense of data as a way of knowing the world and turning it into a point of intervention. They challenge and change the mainstream politics of knowledge, and operate as mediators between the dominant "algorithmic culture" (Striphas 2015) and the citizenry at large. They operate as a "critical community" composed of "critical thinkers who have developed a sensibility to some problem, an analysis of the sources of the problem, and a prescription for what should be done". These critical thinkers "seek acceptance of a new conceptualisation of a problem [...] [and] attempt to influence the conceptual framework used to think about a cluster of issues" (Rochon 1998: 22–23).

For its rich history of uncovering the politics and partiality of technology and scientific knowledge (Winner 1980; Haraway 1988), STS can help to understand fully grasp the potential of the alternative epistemic cultures of data activism. STS shows that science and technology are neither purely technical nor social, but are co-produced through very specific settings that bring along particular (material) affordances, situated practices, and tacit knowledge. This means that values and modes of working stemming from these settings become *inscribed* in the way science and technology develop. STS scholars have always been interested in what happens when the range of actors participating in this process of co-production is stretched up. They have paid attention to these arguably democratic moments in which various actors have influenced technological development, for example through the study of activist appropriations of science and technology by patient movements (Epstein 1995) or technology activists (Hess 2005). We propose two possible focus areas for an STS analysis of the alternative epistemic cultures of data activism.

STS has explained how particular objects and methods that traditionally belong to the epistemic community and culture of scientists and experts have been opened up to a different population, sometimes in democratically designed settings, and how along this trajectory these objects and methods have been malleable to change. For example, Epstein's study (1995) on clinical trials on HIV patients showed how the mainstream scientific epistemology can be altered by the emergence of a grassroots, alternative one. The protocol for clinical trials wanted these to be conducted on a clean population with no prior medicine use. But clinical trials were among the few ways HIV patients could get access to treatment. Patients contested this practice on the ground that it did not mirror the "real world", given only few individuals had a clean history of medicine use. A group of patients resorted to scientific literature to educate themselves, constructing novel discourses about clinical trials. An alternative epistemic culture emerged in which up-and-coming knowledge and arguments collided with the official values and discourses concerning access to medicine. Eventually, the patients managed to have their alternative epistemology taken serious. Epstein's analysis provides a valuable lesson for observers of citizens' responses to datafication: in a context in which "big data" becomes an important reference point for "new" ways of knowing, one can track alternative data narratives and emerging forms and dynamics of counter-expertise.

STS are also known for mobilizing a particular vocabulary and method by carefully tracing how science and technology develop through sociotechnical assemblages. Especially scholars of Actor Network Theory (ANT) – which treats objects like machines as part of heterogeneous networks with humans – have argued that the material agency of artifacts should not be neglected (Callon 1986; Akrich 1992; Latour 2005). In later works, ANT scholars have also tackled the issue of the democratic agency of things and have probed the exploratory question of what could be the potential of their democratic agency (Latour 2005; Latour and Weibel 2005; Marres 2011). In his *Politics of Nature* (2004), Latour designed a "parliament of things" in which he outlined how proper representation of "things" would look like, repurposing rather classic notions of representation and voice. Focusing instead on "issue politics" (Marres 2005), Marres (2011) looked at how material devices participate in the "articulation of issues". In her view, everyday material devices facilitate the articulation of concerns because they provide particular logics for action and for dealing with problems. Material devices therefore contribute to what we understand as matters for the public, and shape our social behavior, too. An era in which we see "data inscriptions" everywhere around us, be it through narratives based on numbers or data visualisations and infrastructure, there is a real need for a critical look at the agency gained (or lost) by and through these inscriptions.

STS thus helps us, on the one hand, to zoom in on the participation of new critical actors in knowledge generation and, on the other, to appreciate the political and potential democratic impact of the material agency enshrined in data, algorithms and infrastructure. Both appear very relevant for our exercise of understanding how new epistemic data cultures shape up. If we consider data not as something given but as a *techne*, i.e. a form of "making" as argued above, we ought to take these critical forms of data making seriously.

Data activism as a heuristic tool

We argue that data activism constitutes a valuable heuristic tool for the study of political participation and civil engagement in the age of datafication, a sort of "lens" through which one can investigate how activism evolves in relation to big data. Data activism is a composite, polyfunctional, holistic and polysemic notion. First, it is a composite concept because, as its interdisciplinary origin suggests, it is made of parts: at the minimum people, (variably sustained forms of) contention, information, and technology. Second, it is polyfunctional, as it can be read through diverse disciplinary lenses, and can be domesticated to investigate different dynamics and relations, between and within people, information, technology, and the state/industry complex. Third, data activism encourages us to adopt a holistic perspective, as it allows us to bring under the same umbrella the two facets of the "data revolution": the productive and the harmful qualities of the "big data" phenomenon, the opportunities and the threats brought forward by datafication, as well as the varied response of the grassroots, be it recognition or resistance. By taking data activism as a whole, we are able to bypass these dichotomies, acknowledging that they ultimately adhere to the same phenomenon of data countercultures/practices, whose components cannot be fully understood if taken in isolation. Finally, as a consequence of its holistic nature, the notion of data activism is polysemic, since "activism" embraces practices of resistance and instances of appropriation as discrete but complementary means to achieving political goals, allowing very distinct attitudes towards institutions and social norms to coexist.

As a heuristic device of sociological nature, data activism is simultaneously flexible and specific enough as to guide and support the analysis of a multifaceted empirical phenomenon where the "social" dimension of taking action (i.e., mobilising and organising) is mediated by the "technical" of information and technology. However, the notion has yet to enter in conversation with the empirical field, and thus can be considered in its guise of theoretical construct, or "the consequence[s] of theories or conventions" that "exist[s] primarily to serve the interest of investigators" (Ragin 1992: 8). This does not deny the existence of empirical units out there. On the contrary, it affirms that these (and especially the borders defining them) are the consequence of the researchers' choice on the basis of theoretical considerations and empirical intuitions. In this respect, we expect the theoretical category of data activism to "coalesce in the course of the research. Neither empirical or given, [it is] gradually imposed on empirical evidence" (Ragin 1992: 10). In sum, the notion can be seen both as a product of the attempt to define the object of investigation by connecting two approaches, respectively resistance and engagement, that might not be necessarily or explicitly connected by activists themselves; and a working hypothesis susceptible to contestation, revision and refinement in the course of the research.

The collective action dimension of data activism at the hearth of this notion can be best analysed using the conceptual toolkit of social movement studies. In what follows, we provide suggestions for the operationalisation of data activism as a heuristic tool, engaging in an exercise of preliminary mapping based on desk research as well as Milan's earlier studies on radical tech activism (Milan 2013; 2015a), which bears some resemblance to data activism.

Zooming in on the many ways in which individuals and groups engage with data politics, we identify two main approaches: datafication is interpreted as a challenge to individual rights *or* as a novel set of opportunities for advocacy and social change. This translates into a varied action repertoire, i.e. the range of tactics activists may adopt to pursue their goals (Taylor/Van Dyke 2004), that is positioned along a continuum between two kinds of responses that are not necessarily in contradiction with each other: contentious attitudes such as obfuscating and resisting vs. embracing and making the most of datafication. Under the data activism umbrella we therefore identify and assemble at least two forms of action repertoires that are often considered as antithetical. Those activists who perceive massive data collection as a threat to their values, freedoms and activities, often use technical means like encryption or anonymity networks to resist monitoring by state and corporations. We understand this approach as "*re*-active data activism", underscoring the fact that activists react to exogenous threats trying to defend their values, beliefs and practices and/or undermine those dynamics and mechanisms they reject. On the opposite end of the spectrum we position those activists who consider the increasing availability of data as an unprecedented, powerful opportunity to provoke social change. They create, mobilise, solicit, appropriate, or crunch data in view of supporting alternative narratives of the social reality, questioning the truthfulness of other representations, denouncing injustice and advocating for change. We label this form of data activism "*pro*-active", in order to highlight how activists take charge and engage in hands-on practices of appropriation and re-use. "Reactive" and "proactive" represents two facets of the same phenomenon: both take information as a constitutive force in society capable to shape social reality (Braman 2009). Analytically, these labels constitute ideal-types: while they are guilty of approximation and generalisation, they serve the purpose of drawing attention to what various approaches to data activism might have in common.

When we look at action repertoires, we can detect some similarities with other technology-oriented movements (Hess 2005) and subcultures. Like the open-source movement, data activism might concern the promotion of alternative technologies and shaping the surrounding policies; sometimes this might entail some form of collaboration with the industry (ibid.). This is particularly true amongst proactive data activists, when they engage in software development or collaborate with state institutions. Reactive data activists, on the contrary, tend to uphold an adversarial attitude towards the state/industry complex; their action repertoire, which includes self-defence, civil disobedience and disruption, is inspired to the radical tech activists of the early days (Milan 2013). Both share the hands-on approach that postulates first-person engagement with information and technology seen as objects of intervention.

The selection of tactics, however, is known to reflect the activists' cultural and ideological preferences (Milan 2013). Some data activists share the "engineering philosophy to 'make things work'" of open source developers, coupled with a certain "insistence on adopting a technocratic approach to solving societal problems and to bypassing ('hacking') legislative approaches" (Berry 2008: 102). Ideologically, though, data activists appear to cover a broad ground, from the self-organisation and -determination of anarchism to anti-state anarcho-capitalism tendencies, to an emphasis on transparency and openness to one on human rights, social justice and the fight against inequality. The notion of collective identity can help us mapping ideological and cultural inclinations, the way they are built, reproduced and maintained over time. Collective identity refers to the process through which "a collective becomes a collective" (Melucci 1996: 84): a sort of "esprit de corps" (Blumer 1939) that holds people together. Some data activists are characterised by a "technical identity", which is suggestive of a closer relationship with technology than that of lay users (Dunbar-Hester 2012). Unitary and adversarial ideas of democracy often coexist, bearing distinct ideological preferences that have consequences, for instance preventing collaboration with state institutions. Certainly, data activism as a whole still lacks a collective identity of its own, visible for example in the fact that only seldom do activists define themselves primarily as "data activists".

Finally, data activism concerns both individuals and groups, as taking action does not necessarily call for a collectivity to mobilise as well. Many contentious actions in data activism are performed at the individual level: think, for example, of engaging in programming or inserting data into a spreadsheet. While it is mainly the group that takes action, and it takes peer-to-peer recognition and interaction to give meaning to action, individual acts of data activism like encrypting private communication do matter, because "there is protest even when it is not part of an organised movement" (Jasper 1997: 5).

Towards a research agenda on data activism

Cycling back to where we started, we can revisit the introductory examples in light of our reflections on data activism. The first two cases represent instances of proactive data activism, while the third represents both. *La Cura* engages in a sort of big-data update of the patient activism described by Epstein. Faced with the enclosure of medical knowledge, Iaconesi managed to lay the ground for an innovative epistemic culture in which the values of openness and collaboration were inscribed into the discourses and practices of health data. His hack enriched the action repertoire by bringing technology and alternative data cultures to bear on "official" knowledge discourses. By repurposing OSINT, otherwise usually associated with intelligence services, and offering trainings and tools to perform investigative data journalism, Bellingcat activists engage in a public learning experiment inspired to open source principles (cf. Glassman and Kang 2012). Apps like CameraV, built to facilitate the uptake of image material in evidential arenas, perform data activism by carefully curating metadata. Here the (encrypted) storage and formatting of data becomes a socio-technical configuration accommodating particular causes (cf. van der Velden 2015). These cases constitute data activism because they *question data agency*, inviting other people to produce their own data inscriptions and to actively "shape issues" in the datafied society, meanwhile contributing to the creation of alternative epistemologies of what data means and represents. But they raise questions, too: how do activists make "data count"? In other words, how do they determine what constitutes relevant and "true" data? To what extent are these "critical" approaches to datafication? How do we draw the line between critique and positivism?

In this article, we suggested that data activism supports the emergence of novel epistemic cultures within civil society, contributing alternative narratives of our datafied social reality. We offered the notion of data activism as a heuristic tool to study citizens' engagement with datafication, emphasizing data activism as an evolving theoretical construct – a working hypothesis susceptible to contestation and revision throughout the empirical research. But how might a research agenda on data activism look like?

Potential questions address both the emerging ontologies and epistemologies of data activism as an empirical phenomenon. Thinking about ontologies of data activism implies investigating the nature of collective action in grassroots data politics, by means of naming and defining of types, properties and interrelations. To this end, we proposed a first typology of data activism that situates two seemingly contradictory approaches – proactive engagements with data (e.g., data-based advocacy) and reactive attitudes (e.g., using and developing encryption tools) – in a continuum that encapsulates the nuanced grassroots responses to the fundamental paradigm shift imposed by datafication. We might then ask who is involved in particular practices of data making (or, in STS vocabulary, who are the main actors and what are the implications of this composition?) How do technical practices, social values and ideologies play out in these emergent alternative epistemic cultures? What kinds of practices are performed to make these alternative data and narratives count? (In other words, how are questions of relevance, truth or political goals determined, and do these decisions connect to technical affordances of, e.g., analytics tools?) Do the activists differ from the state or the industry in the way they treat and mobilise data? How do data activists influence the agenda of other movements? How do they incorporate reflections on gender, privilege, digital labour? What does "critical engagement" mean in the context of data activism?

We should also ask higher-order questions concerning the interplay between data activism and datafication, and between data activism and the evolution of democracy more in general. How is data constructed or enacted, and what values and modes of understandings are inscribed in this process? (How is data "co-produced"?). What are the political and democratic possibilities of data? How do data and data activism partake in shaping larger societal issues, and how do they affect our behaviour in relation to those? What lessons might data activism hold for contemporary social movements and the citizenry at large? How does data activism contribute to (re-)define the ways we think citizenship, engagement, and democratic deliberation and participation?

But the assumption that activist data interventions express articulations of unfolding alternative epistemic cultures interrogates our modes of knowing about data activism in itself, calling for a reflection on research epistemology and triggering a set of meta-questions that query and situate the key role of researchers in labelling and interpreting social reality. We consider reflecting on our own epistemologies as a moral imperative, if we are to respect grassroots data politics and the activists' effort to question dominant narratives and ways of knowing the world. For example, what constitutes "critical" data practices, and who and how sets the parameters for assessing such critique and its validity? This contemplation of research epistemologies must go hand in hand with methodological questions concerning our engagement with the field. What are the key moments for investigating data activism? (In an STS fashion, what is the "controversial" moment when data epistemic cultures get interrupted and reorganised?) What methods are the most conducive to the investigation of data activism practices? What new, participatory methods can we envision, which can best incorporate the criticism to dominant epistemologies of knowing advanced by data activism? Are there ways to do *data-activist research* and what is specific to them? We define data-activist research as a type of co-generative inquiry and a way of conducting "engaged research" (Milan 2014) that turns (research) data into points of intervention, supporting grassroots efforts. To envisage how data-activist research might look like, how it might be practiced, and whether it is desired at all, is a challenging task for both the research and the activist community.

References

Akrich, Madeleine (1992): "The De-Scription of Technical Objects." In: Wiebe E. Bijker/John Law (eds.), Shaping Technology/Building Society. Studies in Sociotechnical Change, Cambridge, MA: MIT Press, pp. 205–24.

Aouragh, Miriyam/Gürses, Seda/Rocha, Jara/Snelting, Femke (2015): "Let's First Get Things Done! On Division of Labour and Techno-Political Practices of Delegation in Times of Crisis." In: Fiberculture 26, pp. 208–35.

Baack, Stefan (2015): "Datafication and Empowerment: How the Open Data Movement Re-Articulates Notions of Democracy, Participation, and Journalism." In: Big Data & Society 2/2, pp. 1–11.

Bennett, Lance W. (2012): "The Personalisation of Politics: Identity, Social Media, and Changing Patterns of Participation." In: The Annals of the American Academy 644, pp. 20–39.

Bennett, Lance W./Segerberg, Alexandra (2013): The Logic of Connective Action: Digital Media and the Personalisation of Contentious Politics, Cambridge, UK: Cambridge University Press.

Berry, David M. (2008): Copy, Rip, Burn: The Politics of Copyleft and Open Source, London: Pluto Press.

Birchall, Clare (2014): "Radical Transparency?" In: Cultural Studies ↔ Critical Methodologies 17/4, pp. 77–88.

Blumer, Herbet G. (1939): "Collective Behavior." In Robert E. Park (ed.), An Outline of the Principles of Sociology, New York: Barnes & Noble, pp. 221–80.

boyd, dana/Crawford, Kate (2012): "Critical Questions for Big Data. Provocations for a Cultural, Technological, and Scholarly Phenomenon." In: Information, Communication & Society 15/5, pp. 662–79.

Braman, Sandra (2004): "The Meta-Technologies of Information." In: Sandra Braman (ed.), Biotechnology and Communication: The Meta-Technologies of Information, Mahwah, NJ: Lawrence Erlbaum Associates, pp. 3–36.

Braman, Sandra (2009): Change of State: Information, Policy, and Power, Cambridge, MA: MIT Press.

Bruno, Isabelle/Didier, Emmanuel/Prévieux, Julien (2014). Statactivisme. Comment lutter avec des nombres, Paris: La Découverte.

Bruno, Isabelle/Didier, Emmanuel/Vitale, Tommaso (2014): "Statactivism: Forms of Action between Disclosure and Affirmation." In: Partecipazione & Conflitto 7/2, pp. 198–220.

Brunton, Finn/Nissenbaum, Helen (2015): Obfuscation: A User's Guide for Privacy and Protest, Cambridge, MA: MIT Press.

Cairo, Alberto (2012): "Facing the Dataclysm." In: The Functional Art: An Introduction to Information Graphics and Visualisation, San Francisco: New Riders (http://www.thefunctionalart.com/2014/09/facing-dataclysm.html).

Callon, Michel (1986): "Some Elements of a Sociology of Translation: Domestication of the Scallops and the Fishermen of St Brieuc Bay." In: John Law (ed.), Power, Action and Belief: A New Sociology of Knowledge?, London: Routledge, pp. 196–223.

Castells, Manuel (2009): Communication Power, Oxford: Oxford University Press.

Chun, Wendy (2011): Programmed Visions Software and Memory, Cambridge, MA: MIT Press.

Coleman, Gabriella (2013): Coding Freedom: The Ethics and Aesthetics of Hacking, Princeton: Princeton University Press.

Couldry, Nick/Powell, Alison (2014): "Big Data from the Bottom up." In: Big Data & Society 1/2, pp. 1–5.

Cukier, Kenneth/Mayer-Schoenberger, Viktor (2013): "The Rise of Big Data: How It's Changing the Way We Think about the World." In: Foreign Affairs 92/3, pp. 28–40.

Dalton, Craig M./Taylor, Linnet/Thatcher, Jim (2016): "Critical Data Studies: A Dialog on Data and Space." Big Data & Society January-June, pp. 1–9.

Delfanti, Alessandro (2013): Biohackers: The Politics of Open Science, London: Pluto Press.

della Porta, Donatella (1995): Social Movements, Political Violence, and the State, Cambridge, UK: Cambridge University Press.

Downing, John D. H. (ed.) (2011): Encyclopedia of Social Movement Media, Thousands Oaks, CA: Sage.

Dunbar-Hester, Christina (2012): "Soldering Toward Media Democracy: Technical Practice as Symbolic Value in Radio Activism." In: Journal of Communication Inquiry 36/2, pp. 149–169.

Epstein, Steven (1995): "The Construction of Lay Expertise: AIDS Activism and the Forging of Credibility in the Reform of Clinical Trials." In: Science, Technology & Human Values 20/4, pp. 408–437.

Fraser, Nancy (2005): "Reframing Injustice in a Globalizing World." In: New Left Review 36, pp. 69–88.

Gabrys, Jennifer (2016): Program Earth: Environmental Sensing Technology and the Making of a Computational Planet, Minneapolis: University of Minnesota Press.

Ganesh, Maya Indira/Hankey, Stephanie (2015): "From Information Activism to the Politics of Data." In: Fiberculture 26, pp. 275–286.

Gitelman, Lisa (2013): "Raw Data" is an Oxymoron, Cambridge, MA: MIT Press.

Glassman, Michael/Kang, Min Ju (2012): "Intelligence in the Internet Age: The Emergence and Evolution of Open Source Intelligence (OSINT)." In: Computers in Human Behavior 28/2, pp. 673–82.

Gray, Jonathan/Chambers, Lucy/Bounegru, Liliana (eds.) (2012): The Data Journalism Handbook. Sebastopol: O'Reilly.

Gürses, Seda/Kundnani, Arun/Hoboken, Joris van (2016): "Crypto and Empire: The Contradictions of Counter-Surveillance Advocacy." In: Media, Culture & Society 38/4, pp. 576–590.

Haraway, Donna (1988): "Situated Knowledges: The Science Question in Feminism and the Privilege of Partial Perspective." In: Feminist Studies 14/3, pp. 575–599.

Heemsbergen, Luke J. (2014): "Designing Hues of Transparency and Democracy after WikiLeaks: Vigilance to Vigilantes and Back Again." In: New Media & Society 17/8, pp. 1340–1357.

Hellerstein, Joseph (2008): "The Commoditisation of Massive Data Analysis." In: Radar, November 19 (http://strata.oreilly.com/2008/11/the-commoditisation-of-massive.html).

Hess, David J. (2005): "Technology-and-Product-Oriented Movements: Approximating Social Movement Studies and Science and Technology Studies." In: Science, Technology & Human Values 30/4, pp. 515–535.

Iaconesi, Salvatore (2016): "[Air-L] La Cura: Possibilities?" Association of Internet Researchers Mailinglist, May 31 (http://listserv.aoir.org/pipermail/air-l-aoir.org/2016-May/033196.html).

Irwin, Alan (1995): Citizen Science: A Study of People, Expertise and Sustainable Development, London-New York: Routledge.

Jasanoff, Sheila (ed.) (2004): States of Knowledge: The Co-Production of Science and the Social Order, London-New York: Routledge.

Jasper, James M. (1997): The Art of Moral Protest: Culture, Biography, and Creativity in Social Movements, Chicago: Chicago University Press.

Jordan, Tim (2015): Information Politics. Liberation and Exploitation in the Digital Society, London: Pluto Press.

Jordan, Tim/Taylor, Paul (2004): Hackitivism and Cyberwars: Rebels with a Cause?, London-New York: Routledge.

Kitchin, Rob (2014): "Big Data, New Epistemologies and Paradigm Shifts." In: Big Data & Society April–June, pp. 1–12.

Knorr Cetina, Karin/Reichmann, Werner (2015): "Epistemic Cultures." In: International Encyclopedia of the Social & Behavioral Sciences, 2nd ed., New York: Elsevier, pp. 873–80.

Latour, Bruno (2004): Politics of Nature: How to Bring the Sciences into Democracy, Cambridge, MA: Harvard University Press.

Latour, Bruno (2005): Reassembling the Social: An Introduction to Actor-Network-Theory, Oxford: Oxford University Press.

Latour, Bruno/Weibel, Peter (2005): Making Things Public: Atmospheres of Democracy, Cambridge, MA: The MIT Press.

Levy, Steven (1984): Hackers: Heroes of the Computer Revolution, New York: Dell/Doubleday.

Lupton, Deborah (2016): The Quantified Self, New York: Wiley.

Lyon, David (2014): "Surveillance, Snowden, and Big Data: Capacities, Consequences, Critique." In: Big Data & Society 1/2, pp. 1–13.

Lyon, David (2015): Surveillance After Snowden, Cambridge-Malden, MA: Polity Press.

Marres, Noortje (2005): "No Issue, No Public: Democratic Deficits after the Displacement of Politics." PhD Diss., University of Amsterdam (http://dare.uva.nl/record/165542).

Marres, Noortje (2011): "The Costs of Public Involvement: Everyday Devices of Carbon Accounting and the Materialisation of Participation." In: Economy and Society 40/4, pp. 510–33.

Marvin, Carolyn (1990): When Old Technologies Were New: Thinking About Electric Communication in the Late Nineteenth Century, Oxford: Oxford University Press.

Maxigas (2012): "Hacklabs and Hackerspaces – Tracing Two Genealogies." In: Journal of Peer Production 2.

May, Timothy C. (1992): "The Crypto Anarchist Manifesto" (http://www.activism.net/cypherpunk/crypto-anarchy.html).

McCaughey, Martha/Ayers, Michael D. (eds.) (2003): Cyberactivism: Online Activism in Theory and Practice, London-New York: Routledge.

Melucci, Alberto (1996): Challenging Codes. Collective Action in the Information Age, Cambridge, UK: Cambridge University Press.

Milan, Stefania (2013): Social Movements and Their Technologies: Wiring Social Change, Basingstoke: Palgrave Macmillan.

Milan, Stefania (2014): "The Ethics of Social Movement Research." In: Donatella della Porta (ed.), Methodological Practices in Social Movement Research, Oxford: Oxford University Press, pp. 446–464.

Milan, Stefania (2015a): "Hacktivism as a Radical Media Practice." In: Chris Atton (ed.), Routledge Companion to Alternative and Community Media, New York: Routledge, pp. 550–60.

Milan, Stefania (2015b): "When Algorithms Shape Collective Action: Social Media and the Dynamics of Cloud Protesting." In: Social Media and Society 1/2, pp. 1–10.

O'Brien, Paraic (2013): "Brown Moses: The British Blogger Tracking Syrian Arms." In: Channel 4 News, March 30 (http://www.channel4.com/news/brown-moses-blog-syria-arms-weapons-croatia).

Ragin, Charles C. (1992): "Introduction: Cases of 'What Is a Case?'" In: Charles C. Ragin/Howard Saul Becker (eds.), What Is a Case? Exploring the Foundations of Social Inquiry, Cambridge, UK: Cambridge University Press, pp. 1–15.

Renzi, Alessandra/Langlois, Ganaele (2015): "Data Activism." In: Greg Elmer/Ganaele Langlois/Joanna Redden (eds.), Compromised Data: From Social Media to Big Data, London: Bloomsbury, pp. 202–25.

Rochon, Thomas R. (1998): Culture Moves. Ideas, Activism, and Changing Values, Princeton: Princeton University Press.

Russon Gilman, Hollie (2016): Participatory Budgeting and Civic Tech: The Revival of Citizen Engagement, Washington, DC: Georgetown University Press.

Schrock, Andrew R. (2016): "Civic Hacking as Data Activism and Advocacy: A History from Publicity to Open Government Data." In: New Media & Society 18/4, pp. 581–99.

Sifry, Micah L. (2011): Wikileaks and the Age of Transparency, New York: OR Books.

Sismondo, Sergio (2003): An Introduction to Science and Technology Studies, Malden, MA: Wiley-Blackwell.

Striphas, Ted (2015): "Algorithmic Culture." In: European Journal of Cultural Studies 18/4-5, pp. 395–412.

Tactical Tech Collective (2013): Visualising Information for Advocacy, Bangalore: Tactical Tech Collective.

Tactical Tech Collective (2016): "Decoding Data." In: Exposing The Invisible, October 18 (https://exposingtheinvisible.org/guides/decoding-data/).

Taylor, Verta/van Dyke, Nella (2004): "'Get Up, Stand Up': Tactical Repertoires of Social Movements." In: David A. Snow/Sarah A. Soule/Hanspeter Kriesi (eds.), The Blackwell Companion to Social Movements, Malden, MA and Oxford: Blackwell, pp. 262–93.

The Guardian Project (n.d.): "CameraV: Secure Verifiable Photo & Video Camera" (https://guardianproject.info/apps/camerav/).

Van der Velden, Lonneke (2015): "Forensic Devices for Activism: Metadata Tracking and Public Proof." In: Big Data & Society 2/2.

Van Dijck, José (2013): The Culture of Connectivity: A Critical History of Social Media, Oxford: Oxford University Press.

Winner, Langdon (1980): "Do Artifacts Have Politics?" In: Daedalus 109/1, pp. 121–36.

Zuboff, Shoshana (2015): "Big Other: Surveillance Capitalism and the Prospects of an Information Civilisation." In: Journal of Information Technology 30/1, pp. 75–89.

Simondon on Datafication
A Techno-Cultural Method

Mark Coté, Jennifer Pybus

Abstract

This article proposes the techno-cultural workshop as an innovative method for opening up the materiality of computational media and data flows and order to increase understanding of the socio-cultural and political-economic dimensions of datafication. Building upon the critical, creative hacker ethos of technological engagement, and the collective practice of the hackathon, the techno-cultural workshops is directed at humanities researchers and social and cultural theorists. We conceptually frame this method via Simondon as a practice-led opportunity to rethink the contested relationship between the human, nature and technology, with a view to challenging social and cultural theory that ignores the human reality of the technical object. We outline an exemplar techno-cultural workshop which explored mobile apps as i) an opportunity to use new digital tools for empirical research, and ii) as technical objects and elements for better understanding their social and cultural dimensions. We see political efficacy in the techno-cultural method not only in augmenting critical and creative agency, but as a practical exploration of the concept of data technicity, an inexhaustible relationality that exceeds the normative and regulatory utility of the data we generate and can be linked anew into collective capacities to act.

Keywords: Datafication; hacker; digital materiality; data technicity.

Introduction

Hackathons have been riding the wave of the data deluge, growing from a niche event for programmers and software developers to an established techno-cultural phenomenon with foci ranging from social justice issues to corporate profit. Related but not limited to the hackathon is the subject of the hacker, defined by the 1993 Internet Users' Glossary as a person that "delights in having an intimate understanding of the internal workings of a system, computers and computer networks in particular" (Malkin and Parker 1993: 21). This paper draws on both the practice of the hackathon and subject of the hacker to ask after the data deluge, what? That is, now that processes of datafication (Cukier/Mayer-Schonberger 2013; Pybus et al. 2015) have suffused everyday life, transforming how we understand ourselves and the world around us, and increasingly articulating our conditions of possibility in ever-more real time, what can we do to gain data agency? Here we pose a political question: can the interlocking practice and subject of hacking exceed their traditional parameters to strategically counter the tendency toward control and value extraction, which increasingly dominates processes of datafication?

Through a series of externally-funded research projects, we have engaged with hackers and in hackathons. Such experiences have evinced an emerging methodology for critical and active engagement in our material conditions of datafication. By collaborating with coders or programmers, we have been able to draw on their preexisting understanding of the technical processes of datafication. This fulcrum point has enabled us to propose a more heterogeneous, interdisciplinary subject and practice. We therefore, put forward not the hackathon but the interdisciplinary workshop as a *techno-cultural method*. For us, this functions as a zone of translation, a space manifested through different levels in participant skill sets, areas of expertise, and technical capacities. This admixture of participants, some more adept at theorising and others more so at engaging with the material conditions that support and expand the capture of data, enables a new technologically mediated method. Specifically, one that demonstrates how theoretical understanding emerges through and from practical engagement.

We will detail one such workshop that was led by an academic coder-researcher and a prominent white-hat hacker,[1] and attended primarily by arts and humanities students without advanced computer skills. The aim of this techno-cultural workshop was to open up applications in an Android environment and reveal how permissions are written into code, in turn facilitating the myriad and intensive flows of data through to third parties and data brokers. This heterogeneous interdisciplinarity cultivated different pedagogical practices and hence new digital literacies for our participants. In this instance, people shared or developed skill sets for decompiling – or reverse engineering – mobile apps. This technical examination of application source code revealed the permissions written into the software that regularly captures our data. For other participants, the workshop was a collective opportunity for exploring the mode of existence of the very technical objects which enable the processes of datafication. In other words, the processes that transform and produce new forms of value within the mobile ecosystem. We thus propose the interdisciplinary workshops as an emergent *techno-cultural* political space to open other possibilities for critical engagement, by facilitating new practices for understanding those digital objects that enable the capture of our social data so that it can be transformed into multiple sites of surplus value.

---

1   The term 'white hat' is often used to denote a security expert who has been paid to discover various vulnerabilities that may be present with an organisation's software (Zetter 2016).

We are positioning our interdisciplinary workshops under the theoretical paradigm of the philosopher of technology Gilbert Simondon (Bardin 2016; Barthélémy 2015; Combes 2013; MacKenzie 2012; Simondon 1958). His basic article of faith was that the relationship between technology and culture was confused and conflictual, and indeed, one wherein the latter acted as a defensive bulwark against the former, and thus precluded an informed engagement with the human-technical milieu in which we live. We call this a techno-cultural method because, as Simondon noted in the opening paragraphs of his major work, *Du mode d'existence des objets techniques* (1958), there is human reality in technical reality for which the cultural must reckon in knowledge and values. In other words, modes of existence are human and technical in ways that are always already mutually constitutive.[2]

So in addition to developing tools and skills for data practice, we see possibilities in the workshop as a techno-cultural antidote which can recalibrate theoretical engagement with the social, cultural, political and economic dimensions of big data. We posit that 'handling' the technical objects of datafication allow participants to gain a more practical appreciation of how technology resists reduction to discourse and signification because it always already conditions them (Mackenzie 2002: 5). As such, the techno-cultural method exceeds the discursive critiques of cultural theory. Here one might ask how a more direct engagement in technical objects effectively grounds the theorising of techno-cultural relations? The Simondonian inflection on the interdisciplinary workshop makes visible the specific *modes of existence* rooted in the flow of data that we continuously generate. We see political stakes in this critical elaboration of technical culture. Indeed, this opening up or unpacking the technical objects of datafication continues critical inquiry into the 'black box' (Latour 1999), that is, making more visible complex technical systems. What is new is the Simondonian perspective: exposed are technical elements, held together by the dynamic of technicity which coheres disparate realities into technical objects. Significantly, it is also this technicity which articulates the possibilities of collective life. By critically exploring datafication through the technical object of the mobile ecosystem, the interdisciplinary workshop offers a fresh understanding of how it mediates relations between both humans and the environment but also between individuals and collectives.

We present the interdisciplinary workshop as an emergent methodology most appropriate to our era of ubiquitous datafication. Amidst processes which quantify, calculate, qualify, classify, categorise and otherwise produce knowledge about ourselves and the world around us in an increasingly real-time and pre-cognitive manner, we see possibilities for a different methodology, capable of providing ways of engaging in the digital ecosystems that make up our everyday lives. By foregrounding our human and technical modes of existence in their complex

---

2   "Nous voudrions montrer que la culture ignore dans la réalité technique une réalité humaine, et que, pour jouer son role complet, la culture doit incorporer les êtres techniques sous forme de connaissance et de sens des valeurs." (Simondon 1958: 9)

unfolding relations, we question whether we can more rigorously understand how the human, in its social, cultural political and economic dimensions is only ever mediated by and exteriorised through technical objects. We do so by first concisely outlining the hacker and hackathons, a subjectivity and practice we both draw upon and break from. What of their situated specificity can be diffused into an open and generalised critical and creative interdisciplinary environment to match the challenges of pervasive and proprietary datafication? We will then outline an exemplar interdisciplinary workshop that we held which explored the mobile ecosystem. Finally, we pass this approach through the Simondonian prism to see if we can effectively present a social pedagogy of technics.

Hacker and Hackathons

The techno-cultural workshop draws from both the hacker and hackathons, even though we lay claim to representing neither in our proposed method. Instead, we are situating our proposal of the techno-cultural workshop in relation to the diverse ways that different hacker communities aspire to engage and transform technologies as political practices. These might include the creation and circulation of free software (Kelty 2008; Coleman 2012), the cultivation of myriad forms of participatory and tinkerer cultures (Wark 2005; Ratto/Boler 2014) as well as a political commitments to openness and interoperability (Baack 2015; Powell 2012), that is, to making accessible what otherwise might remain opaque to the everyday user. We agree with Kelty that "coding, hacking, patching, sharing, compiling, and modifying of software are forms of political action" (2008: 8). Where we differ, however, is in imagining these capacities as becoming diffused beyond the geek by turning the workshop into both an intermediary and a site of collaboration and learning between hackers and non-hackers. Such emerging collectives can cultivate more widespread understanding of our "unruly technical materiality" (2008: 8) that infuses our own data making practices. Our contention is that the workshop can unpack not only the material objects that seek to capture our own socio-cultural practices when we use applications but how that mode of technical existence engenders – that is, enables and constrains – subsequent modes of human existence. This is why we are drawn to practices that drive the social imaginaries of geeks, as there we see tools that can prise open an array of black boxes through which we collectively live.

The hackathon holds interest as a spatio-temporally defined event, an assemblage with broad methodological possibilities. For example, we have used them to create different tools to facilitate a more data literate subject,[3] or, as outlined here, to break open the proprietarily guarded and siloed ecosystems of our various

---

3   For a more detailed account, please see our previous article 'Hacking the Social Life of Big Data' (Pybus/Coté/Blanke 2015).

platforms and devices. Traditionally, these events are structured on an established trajectory, as outlined by Lodato and DiSalvo (2016). First, the participants are presented with a series of challenges from which they will have to choose; next they will organise themselves into teams, ideally possessing an array techno-capacities – including both front and backend skills; and, finally, often after two days (and lots of pizza),[4] participants will present the digital objects that they have created to the larger group. These punctuated moments of creative productivity generate forms of value that are both contested and difficult to measure. On the one hand, the events yield prototypes and tools as a result of group creation. We are in agreement with Lodato and DiSalvo however, that the value of the hackathon cannot be distilled down to what was produced but instead to the mode of material participation itself (2016). Indeed, it is the structure of the event that draws various human and material elements together wherein we see critical and creative possibilities. In other words, we see a potential in the process and means by which participation is enacted which is more important than the outcome. Others, such as Gregg (2015), frame these events as exploitative sites of immaterial or 'free' labor, focusing on the productive outcomes, as opposed to the process. As an Intel-based researcher, she limits her focus to corporate hackathons, which the high-tech industry use as an important site of capture, drawing on employee goodwill and general intellect, and in the process augmenting their productivity while extracting surplus value. Gregg, however, dismisses any political possibility within the hackathon as a "momentary exercises in speculative citizenship"(2015: 195) that only bring about a theoretical win and subsequently, acts to further normalise the solitary conditions of economic insecurity.

We do not take issue with this critique of the often calculated corporate practice of hackathons. Gregg's eagerness to disavow this practice, however, assumes that those power-knowledge relations embedded within capitalist working relations are both fixed and reified, sidelining any possibility of struggle that arguably exists within the means of production or in this case the hackathon as a modality of participation. Yet, technologically-engaged participation is the cohesive dynamic in the hacker ethos as outlined in Levy's (1984) tenants. And while Gregg's corporate example gives credence to Kelty's (2008) charge that elements of the hacker ethos can become a reified norm from a now past historical moment, this does not require a disavowal of collective technical action. Simondon (1958) stresses the importance of collective techno-cultural action. He would not dispute the gravity of estrangement from the means of production, which Gregg puts forward by proxy with the hackathon.[5] However, Simondon fundamentally differs, insofar as

---

4 Often hackathon extend over two days. Those undertaken in our research – namely in the *Our Data Ourselves* project – took place over only one day.
5 Simondon would likely agree insofar as he acknowledges the need for "offsetting that form of alienation that occurs in the very interior of the development of technology, following the specialization that society demands and produces." (Simondon 1958: 101)

he refuses to reduce technology to being primarily a tool of production. Elements of a technical object always have potential – an *excess* – beyond their situated utility. This is the crux of his critique of a reductive cultural understanding of technology; indeed, he considers this misapprehension to be a crucial source of alienation. In this way, machine-induced alienation is also a cultural alienation.

Barthélémy clarifies the culpability of culture in our alienation from technology: "it is the culture itself that feels the consequences of an ignorance by which it had defined itself as a work-based culture" (2010: 248). Instead, he argues that we need to liberate the machine and to do so, culture needs to understand technology not only through but beyond labour. What this requires is a different relationship to technology itself, seeing that in addition to being a tool of labour and exploitation, there is also a techno-human capacity for the translation, the conversion, the transduction of disparate potentials and realities. Simondon posits the need for a different understanding of technology to enable new kinds of inter-human relationships, for becoming something *other than*. Such transductions all require collective endeavours of technical invention, and it here that we posit one of many possible roles for the techno-cultural workshop.

Practicing Techno-Culture

On a spring day in 2015, we held a six-hour workshop at King's College London. Participants ranged from hackers, computer scientists, humanities scholars, undergraduate students and interested members of the public. The backgrounds of the 21 participants was extremely diverse, each with varying capacities in relation to computing, reading code and engagement with open source software. The workshop was orchestrated to reach a wide and disparate set of publics through an open invitation that explicitly welcomed all levels of expertise. Furthermore, ongoing support was promised to those lacking computer and/or data literacies skills to enable them to discover and unpack the basic movement of data that is continuously extracted by Android mobile applications. The aim of this session was not to transform novices into experts but to create an environment wherein all participants could i) gain a deeper understanding of the permission protocols embedded in all application housed in the Google Play Store; ii) create a pedagogical space that inspired the "messiness of methods" (Law/Urry 2004: 390) so participants could collectively consider the diverse ways in which their own data assemblages shape their ontological conditions by using pre-rooted Android phones; and iii) consider ways of reconfiguring the data by empowering those with limited technological skills to gain insight into the mechanisms that facilitate the collection and distribution of their data. Overall, we hoped to cultivate more agency and transparency, opening up the black box of the otherwise opaque complex technical networks comprising mobile applications.

Similar to Ruppert, Law and Savage (2013) we were interested in the methodological possibilities that can render visible how data articulate relationships between the cultural, social and material. The workshop, therefore represented more than just an instrumental gathering of bodies with a task at hand, but instead functioned as a site of action based research. Thus, in line with Kennedy et al. (2015: 176) we see possibilities for "an intimate relationship between scholarly inquiry and practical or political activity or intervention" in the social data we routinely produce when using mobile applications. Indeed, we hoped to empower participants to actively understand how apps gather data by directly engaging and discovering aspects of their material infrastructure. By so doing, we created a temporary data public, echoing what Kelty (2008) calls a recursive public. However, unlike with his recursive model, most of our participants were not geeks (although some were) and our objective was not to *create* but rather to *discover* those technical objects and make them accessible for critical use. It is also important to note how the composition of this workshop arose organically through a series of earlier hackathons in our research projects. Initially, we focused exclusively on teen hackers but later when re-deploying this method for post graduate and undergraduate students without the requisite skill sets, we recognised the merit in a more diverse and inclusive collective.

The 'Hacking the Mobile Ecosystem' workshop was designed and led by Giles Greenway and Daryn Martin as a part of our AHRC project which explored the datafication of mediated youth cultural and social practices on mobile platforms.[6] The workshop was inspired by a key finding in the *Our Data Ourselves* project, regarding the irregular data activity of one of the applications – Line Keep In – used by two of our participants. According to our findings, this application had a data flow 35 times higher than the other applications we examined (Pybus et al. 2015). Upon inspecting the code, we found several embedded tools gathering deep statistics and pushing user messages, in addition to a much broader range of permissions seeking personal data access. The outcome from this more traditional hackathon prompted us to pursue further research questions such as: How are apps coding to access data? What is the average amount of data apps access? What kinds of data is accessed? And finally, where does this data actually go? In addition, we also wanted to expand the parameters of the workshop to function as methodological tool. Thus, on the one hand, some participants dug into the source code of the 'Line Keep In' application, and on the other hand, our more inclusive environment enabled non-hackers to explore their own mobile applications via the permissions that facilitate data flows. In this manner, the workshop demonstrated the potential of a truly techno-cultural heuristic method.[7]

---

6   For a more extensive overview please refer to Blanke et al. 2014.
7   Here we used heuristic to denote both a Computer Science definition which signifies a problem solving approach emphasising speed over optimisation, capturing the temporal dimension of a workshop, and for non-expert technological engage-

On the day, participants were given pre-rooted Android phones, which enabled them direct access and control over the operating system and applications that had been installed on the devices they would use in the workshop. Unlocking, rooting or jailbreaking mobiles is a common practice for many hackers or app developers since a rooted device offers complete administrative control, albeit at the cost of voiding the warranty. The workshop introduced the technical elements of rooting a phone as a means for increasing user agency over the operating system and applications on their devices. For example, an unlocked phone can open up unavailable features such as more comprehensive ad blockers, enable users to customise their operating system, or even remove unnecessary software to make more available space. What many of these practices equally enable is the extended life of otherwise old or obsolete phones, thus potentially disrupting the ever-accelerating cycle of mobile phone consumption.

For the majority of workshop participants, this was their first experience exploring the inner workings of an open Android phone operating system, let alone exploring the technical elements of mobile development. Participants were given the task of reverse engineering or decompiling mobile applications which provides access to i) the Android Manifest which defines how an app is structured by including the metadata of all of its components; ii) the list of permissions attached to the Android Manifest which govern the level of access that the application has to user data;[8] iii) the packets of data that pass between the mobile and the server; and iv) for the more advanced, the app's code to determine which third party agreements were present. In order to accomplish these goals, participants downloaded 'virtual machine' (VM) software, which enabled them to run multiple operating systems on their laptop; for example, working within the Android environment while using a MacBook. Greenway and Martin designed a user-friendly VM for participants to augment the capacity of those who were less technologically literate, deploying an array of software which rendered the laptops into inquisitive, critical and creative communication tools, ready to work with rooted, that is, unlocked mobile phones.

There are three key tools worthy of note which enabled this process within the VM. First, the Android Debug Bridge allowed participants to drag mobile applications from the phone onto to their laptops for closer examination. Second, the F/OS reverse engineering tool dex2jar[9] which decompiled the app – that is, broke it

---

ment seeking a critical understanding of the social and cultural dimensions of processes of datafication within a mobile ecosystem. See Bardin (2016) for a related and insightful discussion of heuristic efficacy.

8   The typical user would never actually sees the permissions in the manifest, instead s/he would see the outcome of such permissions as part of the terms and conditions that outline the various ways in which data is accessed and shared by the application.
9   This program makes the information from the Android Manifest visible by translating dex code which is in machine-readable Android bytecode format into jar code, which can then be made human-readable format through a Java decompiler.

open to reveal its technical elements. More specifically, this rendered the machine readable code that programs the application (including the manifest) into more human-friendly Java. Third, the F/OS network packet analyser Wireshark was preloaded to capture and to try and make sense of the data flows. Here, 'Packet sniffing' is a crucial step, which makes visible the normally obfuscated traffic between the application and the server. It is important to note, that the intent of this workshop was not for all participants to drill down to a fine granularity of data flows, although some did; rather, it was to foreground the pedagogical and affective value in actually seeing and experiencing the direct movement of personal data. Within a techno-cultural context, the demystification of this otherwise inaccessible process is highly relevant to all, not simply hackers seeking to modify an application.

A crucial aspect of the techno-cultural workshop is its interdisciplinary bridging, how it is open to different users, goals, tools and their application. Hackers, or just those with more advanced technical skills were able to both dig into data flows governed by an Android Manifest file, as well as subsequently modify the application to their particular needs. But there is a parallel process, a pedagogical space that breaks open datafication processes and thus grounds social and cultural critiques through engagement with the materiality of technical objects. The workshop thus becomes a point of diffusion, not where all become hackers (thus rendering meaningless the specificity of that subjectivity) but where the ethos and practice of critical engagement become open to others. This we see as political, given the aforementioned prominence of datafication in the articulation of contemporary power-knowledge relations. The techno-cultural workshop can function as a temporary collective to help undo divisions between "those who create data [...], those who have the means to collect it, and those who have the expertise to analyze it" (Manovich qtd. in Ruppert 2013: 270). In short, by facilitating temporary data publics, participants can make strange what through habituation is familiar yet unknown and unexamined in practice.

For example, by decompiling the application, participants were able to make visible the permission-based security files of the Android Manifest (AndroidManifest.xml) which governs data flows in and through applications. Some participants decided to examine Facebook's Messenger, and subsequently identified 40 different permissions wherein the application's developer coded legal means for gathering data from its users. So for example, if the user is logged on and sends an MMS message, the Facebook Messenger app or 'Orca' as it is referred in the Android Manifest, states clearly that by so doing, the app can read *all* of the user's texts. In addition, these permissions are also appraised by the Google Play Store, which rates the data gathering practices as being either 'normal', 'dangerous' or 'unknown'. Closer examination of Facebook Messenger revealed that 15 of its permissions were deemed to be 'dangerous'. A small sample of these include:

1. android.permission.ACCESS_COURSE_LOCATION ['dangerous', 'course (networked based) location', 'access location sources, such as the mobile network database, to determine approximate phone location, where available. Malicious applications can use this to determine approximately where you are.'
2. android.permission.CAMERA ['dangerous', 'take pictures and videos', 'Allows application to take pictures and videos with the camera. This allows the application to collect images that the camera is seeing at anytime.']
3. android.permission.SEND_SMS ['dangerous', 'send sms messages', 'Allows application to send SMS messages. Malicious messages may cost you money by sending messages without your confirmation.']

Upon reading the various permissions, our participants made a number of preliminary observations: A) How much clearer the manifest appears in terms of simply listing what data are gathered; B) How useful it was seeing the word 'dangerous', which drew attention to more invasive permissions; C) What does 'unknown' mean? And why is it listed this way?; D) Why does it appear that the Android Manifest appears to be more comprehensive and straightforward than the Terms and Conditions?; E) How might users interact with their apps differently if they had access to the Android Manifest? We regard such observations as crucial moments of translation which invariably arise from any critical techno-cultural engagement. By examining their apps from an entirely different perspective, participants can pose new research questions and open different approaches to critical data literacies.

Further consideration of these preliminary findings might lead us to conclude there is nothing entirely unusual about these permissions, insofar as they ascribe common functionality to apps. Yet, they are also fundamental to calibrating an extensive and intensive flow of personal data which underwrites the data-driven economy. Thus our participants also saw permissions which enabled cross-app and cross-platform data flows, third party access. Such permissions are crucial to the data brokerage ecosystem of marketing and advertising – an area we are examining in ongoing research. Overall, our brief workshop exploration revealed a contrast between the coding and its discursive representation in the Google Play Store. There is an informational disconnect between the banal matter-of-fact detailing of 'dangerous' permissions in the manifest, and the discursive rendering of the 'dangerous' into extended functional features as read by the user. This workshop experiences suggests to us a method open to much more than just the use of new digital tools for learning new data-intensive modes of empirical analysis, although this is one option. What we see is an opportunity to collectively investigate the mechanisms that facilitate the material relays that lead to the capture, spread, movement, and eventual commodification of our mobile data.

Theorising Techno-Cultural Practices

We present the 'Hacking the Mobile Ecosystem' as but one possibility within an emergent practice that we are trying to extend through theoretical reflection. As such, this is very much practice-led theory. In more straightforward terms, we, as non-hackers, first had to explore the hackathon before appreciating its broader critical and creative potential. In this manner, recent research projects have been a journey of discovery through such unfamiliar technology-focused practices. Further, there is a challenge inherent in heterogeneous interdisciplinarity when one enters with a structural deficit in knowledge and capacity. Thus we had to observe and learn about hacking practices so we could meaningfully communicate with coders, programmers and hackers. In working through these interdisciplinary *translation* issues, myriad possibilities oriented around rethinking and re-articulating social and political theory arose through the different ways in which we could engage the technology itself. This translation work, articulating the technical, socio-cultural and political economic, could also be understood through what Simondon calls transduction.

Mackenzie (2002) has an important and eponymous monograph illuminating the dense conceptual thicket underpinning relations between culture and technology. We are drawn by the very idea of transduction, which entails a conveyance and transformation of energy or a signal from one state or domain to another. At risk of oversimplifying, we could say Simondon's core focus was to elucidate points of transduction between technology and culture, between disparate dimensions or realities. In this way, the interdisciplinary workshop as a zone of translation is also one of transduction. Above we outlined how workshops revealed to us the materiality of technical practices of datafication in mobile applications – what Simondon would call the technical object. In turn, this cultivates an understanding of the transductive relations to the cultural and the political. This brings us back to the basic political orientation of the techno-cultural workshop: *an emergent method for critically unpacking the data materiality of the human condition under datafication.*

But why the human condition, or rather human modes of existence under datafication? Given the ubiquity of datafication, we find it opportune to study through a particular realm of the Digital Humanities, the disciplinary domain under which the research projects informing this paper transpired. It is crucial to distinguish, however, that we see this realm not in new computational methodologies for humanities research but rather squarely on the condition of the *digital human* under datafication. Simondon was deeply concerned with the orientation of humanism. Barthélémy (2010) incisively recalls that Simondon gave the name 'facile humanism' to that which ignores the technical object. If we look to the first paragraph of his most significant work: *Du mode d'existence des objects techniques,* Simondon makes clear his intent: to overturn "the assumption that technical objects do not contain human reality" and that "the opposition raised between the cultural and the technical, between the human and machine is false and without foundation" (1958: 9). Barthélémy calls this approach that of a "difficult humanism" (2010: 240) insofar as it integrates human and technical reality, as well as technology into culture. We claim that the techno-cultural workshop practices 'difficult humanism' as it both foregrounds the technical object and enables new examinations of technical life.

It is worth pausing on this point to restate what we propose as especially valuable about the techno-cultural workshop: a practice-led opportunity to rethink the contested relationship between the human, nature and technology, with a view to challenging social and cultural theory that ignores the human reality of the technical object. Barthélémy, on difficult humanism, writes "the technical object is the extension of life through which that life can go beyond itself in a relationship referred to as 'transindividual'" (2010: 49). In other words, technology is the means by which the human, and thus culture, is expressed in nature. If we follow this through, the interdisciplinary workshop as techno-cultural method raises different ontological stakes when the focus becomes the *technical object*. But in order to appreciate the technical object, as presented by Simondon, it is worth quickly contextualising the theoretical paradigm from which it arises.

The very idea that the technical object has a mode of existence, an ontologising capacity or reality, begs the question of its relationship to the human mode of existence. The concept of originary technicity clarifies the calibration of this constitutive relationship by positing that the human and technology were always already linked. Leroi-Gourhan (1993) first popularised the idea of originary technicity in paleo-anthropology in the mid-1960s. His concept frames the shift in the mode of exteriorisation, when proto-hominids first picked up and fashioned rudimentary lithic industry. He posited it as the threshold of the human insofar as it transformed exteriorisation from a biological to a technical tendency. Human culture, thus, is always a technical expression. Derrida (1976) similarly drew on technical exteriorisation in his critique of logocentrism by unsettling the *natural* human and similarly the originary status. Stiegler (1998) also draws on originary technicity in his concept of epiphylogenesis, or the accumulation of experience in technics which in turn impacts upon the very development of the genus homo. Finally, Beardsworth (1996) sees political stakes insofar as originary technicity provides the platform for the differentiation and historicisation human spatio-temporal experience, a focus also taken up by Mackenzie (2002) and Hansen (2004), among others.

Technicity then, is the human condition. Stated otherwise, originary technicity highlights the supplementary nature that was always already human living systems. It is crucial to note that unlike Stiegler, Simondon does not see this supplement as a response to a lack. Instead, technicity is an expression of potential, wherein it manifests *the way life lives*. This means it ontologises, or makes real, a given relationship with the environment as well as enabling forms of social or collective life. Any given technical object – for example, a mobile application – functions to interlace social, political, economic, and cultural dimensions. As such, technicity is crucial for a rigorous understanding of the possibilities of collective life – *the* political task *par excellence*. Here Mackenzie elaborates the techno-cultural stakes: "[T]echnicity refers to a side of collectives which is not fully lived, represented or symbolized, yet which remains fundamental to their grounding, their situation, and the constitution of their limits" (2004: 11).

It is the double articulation of technicity that makes the techno-cultural workshop a method for the 'difficult humanities'. Technicity is both i) the dynamic which coheres the technical object, as well as ii) that which envelopes and articulates the cultural, or the organisation of collective life. In short, it is a method to critically unpack the mode of existence of the datafied human through a two-fold *political* elaboration of technical culture. First, it makes visible constituted power and control, engaging the normative and regulatory dimensions of technical objects which inscribe us more deeply into circuits of production and consumption – for example, in the coded permissions of Facebook Messenger. The second step, however, is crucial insofar as technicity is conceptualised as an excess, a dynamic which always exceeds the purpose or instrumentality of any given technical object. When a technical object is examined with technicity in mind, priority is given to considering how it is always open to something more, for example, coding permissions so data flows as a shared resource, thus differently organising collective life. We contend the double-articulation of technicity lends a political urgency to the techno-cultural method. On the one hand, this method begins examining technical objects of datafication which underpin the political economic commodification of the lifeworld – the social data factory – at unprecedented levels of fine granulation, and which in turn further refine and target mediated content which can distract and dissimulate. On the other hand, the technical object and its constitutive elements can always *become something more* than a regulatory and normative system. This is because its elements are always bound by technicity into a metastable system – that is, supersaturated with potential energy, like a snow-laden mountain slope, pre-avalanche.

Let us briefly consider how our workshop examined apps as a technical object, be it the 'Line Keep In' or 'Facebook Messenger' within the metastable system of datafication, and to consider the technicity cohering its elements. The first point is that life moves beyond itself through the technical object. This is similar to thinking of it as medium wherein nothing remains the same in relation to the technical object, not the sensory-perceptual lived experience of the human, the conditions of possibility of human collectivities, of socio-cultural practices, expressions and organisational forms, labour both in form and in relation to economic value, overarching spatio-temporal calibrations, and, indeed, the environment itself. As we worked through our different hackathons and workshops we found something irresistible about considering any given mobile app as a technical object. For Simondon the technical object is the means by which we are expressed in our lived environment, mediating the human and nature. This gives an innovative frame for the data flows through those applications, which, after all are exteriorisations of the human, of quotidian quanta of everyday life. While we must consider the technicity of such datafication, we must first clarify the techno-cultural method.

Barthélémy reminds us that to ontologise technology – i.e. ascribe to it a mode of existence – is to reject its classification through utility. This is what he calls "the non-anthropological thinking of technology in Simondon" (2015, 51). So a techno-cultural workshop will indeed drill down to the defined use and practical ends of technical objects – namely normalising and regulating the flow of personal data. Yet it can also vet the technicity to consider how that technical object can be rearticulated and open up a vista beyond. For example, to consider permissions as technical elements, which can be modified, is to enact the excess of the technical object beyond the intentionality of its invention or its utility. To restate, the dynamic force binding the myriad elements comprising a given technical object can never be contained in any given social system or use case. Hence the crucial role of technicity. Simondon writes: "technical objects result from an objectification of technicity; they are produced by it, but technicity is not exhausted in objects and is not entirely contained in them either" (1958: 163). As per metastability, technical objects are only ever provisionally stabilised and thus always susceptible to being opened up and their elements reconfigured, becoming something else. The iterability of technical objects comprising the Android mobile ecosystem testifies to this, the fact that it relentlessly commodifies our data notwithstanding. Iterability always marks the technicity adhering a technical object. This capacity to knit together and bring cohesion to diverse elements is why Simondon denotes that technicity functions as "a unity of becoming" (1958: 20) amidst a network of relations.

Technicity always binds a particular set of elements in a grounded situation. It is not a glue to be used once and the tube discarded. As Simondon writes, "technicity is not exhausted in objects and is not entirely contained in them either" (1958: 163). There are two things of note about this super-abundance. As stated, the elements comprising the technical object always contain the potential to become something else. We also suggest there can be a more autonomist reading of technicity, as a kind of constituent power. Such a political reading ascribes a preternatural potential across the modes of existence of the human and the technical. As such, technicity has something of a contestable *hominem ex machina*. This underlines the overarching critical but non-prescriptive political impulse behind the techno-cultural workshop when it enables participants to go beyond the normative regulation of its intended use, and that is the possibilities for other forms of organisation of collective life. As such it is an open method for developing a social pedagogy of technics.

Conclusion

To conclude, the techno-cultural workshop builds on the critical, creative hacker ethos of technological engagement, and the collective practice of the hackathon. We see this as an innovative method for opening up the materiality of computational media and data flows as a way to better grapple with the socio-cultural and political-economic dimensions of datafication. This responds to a call Hansen (2004) made, for the *transcultural* transformation of cultural studies. We see this as a challenge for the techno-cultural theorist: "to become together with technics, to engage in mediations by and with technical objects that place the human in relation to the inhuman, the improper, the preindividual ..." (2004). The techno-cultural workshop is an opportunity to put this into practice and better understand the digital human under datafication. Further, the preindividual resonates with our conceptualisation of the social data we generate: as an *emergent commons*. Indeed, our original hackathons were designed to empower participants to explore that commons, to access their own data for creative and critical use. Here we put forward a provocation, following the Simondonian concept of individuation. What if the techno-cultural workshop helps us think differently of the data we generate? One might be inclined to think of data through Stiegler's (2011) interpretation of tertiary memory. He identifies this with the industrialisation of memory, the kinds of mediating cultural texts one would traditionally associate with the Frankfurt School's culture industry. As evidenced in our workshop's examination of the technical element of permissions, we do know the social and cultural data we generate constitutes a fundamental relationship: it *is* fueling the evolution of commercial digital media and indeed inscribes us ever more seamlessly in circuits of its production and consumption. But one of the prime virtues of a Simondonian frame is that it looks beyond normative and regulatory utility; hence the foregrounding in the techno-cultural method of the excess of technicity. We would add to this another excess: the ever present *constituent power* of the human. This renders our social and cultural data not merely functional for the social data factory but as a possible "means for the human to draw on its preindividual, natural support, which is to say, to persist as an ongoing individuation and to participate in collective transindividuation" (Hansen 2004).

If we think of the data we generate, in terms of its immanent *social life*, it is only already constituted insofar as it is subject to the regulatory and normative applications of capital and the state. In other words, it is the quotidian quanta of already constituted individuals flowing through our mediated social and cultural practices. But that is not all. The unprecedented market value of this data comes from what happens next, after it flows forth into that rich social life of being brokered, aggregated, processed, and analysed in a closed and proprietary system. It then comes back to us, reinscribing the constituted individual with a regulatory and normative force that transpires in an increasingly pre-cognitive temporal mode.

What more can we learn from the techno-cultural method about both the dizzying temporality and non-conscious cognition of technical devices (Hayles 2014) increasingly dominating these flows? For certain there are rich political possibilities in exploring the technicity of this data, a very particular excess manifested in its inexhaustible relationality. The excess of the data we generate is that it can always be linked anew, in collective relations previously unknown. This is the red thread for a techno-cultural workshop. Interventions in the technical ensemble of datafication, opening any given technical object gives us new means to draw on our data, not just to temporarily decompile its regulatory relays, but to directly engage what Simondon calls "the charge of preindividual reality, of this charge of nature that is conserved with the individual being and that contains potentials and virtuality" (1958: 248). Above all else, beings for Simondon are *beings with potential*. Techno-cultural practice composes relays between human and non-human potential, expanding our collective capacity to act. From the modest platform of a mobile ecosystem, we can "construct a new modality of relation, a modality of transductive relation of human to nature and transindividual relation between humans" (Combes 2013: 70). Opening up the flows of our quotidian quanta opens one practical possibility for seeing and forming new relations with what is also a preindividual dimension. Such new relations are crucial to the collective formations of transindividuation, which requires a transduction – a conveyance and transformation – of human and technical elements. Here we concur with Hansen that analysis must become a performance, and, we would add, a practice, "a creative experimentation with the possibilities of our future technogenesis" (2004) which after all, denotes the kinds of relationships we have with technology. Technogenesis, simply, denotes new ways in which life lives through technics.

Under ubiquitous datafication, the technical existence of humans has never been more apparent. But there is, as Combes (2013) reminds us, neither "freedom from" or "mastery over" machines. But what we can do is open the technical system from below. Each time a techno-cultural workshop is enacted, it performs this task. As Bardin and Menegalle (2015) note, this is the crux of Simondon's pedagogical programme: "starting at the reprogramming of individual cognitive capacities towards collective processes of individuation that do not merely resist but invent and experiment in the human techno-symbolic milieu (1958: 16)."

References

Anon. (n.d.): "Cyanogenmod Wiki" (https://wiki.cyanogenmod.org/w/About).
Baack, Stefan (2015): "Datafication and Empowerment: How the Open Data Movement Re-Articulates Notions of Democracy, Participation, and Journalism." In: Big Data & Society 2/2.
Bardin, Andrea (2016): Epistemology and Political Philosophy in Gilbert Simondon, London: Springer.

Bardin, Andrea/Menegalle, Giovanni (2015): "Introduction to Simondon." In: Radical Philosophy: Journal of the Independent Left 189, pp. 15–16.

Barthélémy, Jean-Hugues (2010): "What New Humanism Today?" In: Cultural Politics: An International Journal 6/2, pp. 237–52.

Barthélémy, Jean-Hugues (2015): Life and Technology: An Inquiry Into and Beyond Simondon, Lüneburg: Meson Press.

Beardsworth, Richard (1996): Derrida & the Political, New York: Routledge.

Blanke, Tobias/Greenway, Giles/Pybus, Jennifer/Coté, Mark (2014): "Mining Mobile Youth Cultures." In: IEEE International Conference on Big Data, pp. 14–17 (http://ieeexplore.ieee.org/lpdocs/epic03/wrapper.htm?arnumber=7004447).

Coleman, E. Gabriella (2013): Coding Freedom: The Ethics and Aesthetics of Hacking, Princeton: Princeton University Press.

Combes, Muriel (2013): Gilbert Simondon and the Philosophy of the Transindividual, Cambridge, MA: MIT Press.

Cukier, Kenneth/Mayer-Schonberger, Viktor (2013): Big Data: A Revolution That Will Transform How We Live, Work and Think, London: John Murray.

Derrida, Jacques (1976): Of Grammatology, Baltimore: Johns Hopkins University Press.

Gregg, Melissa (2015): "FCJ-186 Hack for Good: Speculative Labour, App Development and the Burden of Austerity." In: The Fibreculture Journal 25, pp. 183–201.

Hansen, Mark B. N. (2004): "'Realtime Synthesis' and the Différance of the Body: Technocultural Studies in the Wake of Deconstruction." In: Culture Machine 6.

Hayles, N. Katherine (2014): "Cognition Everywhere: The Rise of the Cognitive Nonconscious and the Costs of Consciousness." In: New Literary History 45/2, pp. 199–220.

Kelty, Christopher M. (2008): Two Bits: The Cultural Significance of Free Software, North Carolina: Duke University Press.

Kennedy, Helen/Moss, Giles/Birchall, Christopher/Moshonas, Stylianos (2015): "Balancing the Potential and Problems of Digital Methods through Action Research: Methodological Reflections." In: Information, Communication & Society 18/2, pp. 172–186.

Latour, Bruno (1999): Pandora's Hope: An Essay on the Reality of Science Studies, Cambridge: Harvard University Press.

Law, John/Urry, John (2004): "Enacting the Social." In: Economy and Society 33/3, pp. 390–410.

Leroi-Gourhan, André (1993): Gesture and Speech, Cambridge, MA: MIT Press.

Levy, Steven (1984): Hackers: Heroes of the Computer Revolution, New York: Doubleday.

Lodato, Thomas James/DiSalvo, Carl (2016): "Issue-Oriented Hackathons as Material Participation." In: New Media & Society, 18/4, pp. 539–557.

MacKenzie, Adrian (2002): Transductions: Bodies and Machines at Speed, 1st ed., London: Continuum.

Malkin, Gary/Parker, Tracy (1993): Network Working Group, University of Texas, Austin (http://www.rfc-editor.org/rfc/rfc1392.txt).

Powell, Allison (2012): "Democratizing Production through Open Source Knowledge: From Open Software to Open Hardware." In: Media, Culture & Society 34/6, pp. 691–708.

Pybus, Jennifer/Coté, Mark/Blanke, Tobias (2015): "Hacking the Social Life of Big Data." In: Big Data & Society 2/2, pp. 26–33.

Ratto, Matt/Boler, Megan (2014): DIY Citizenship: Critical Making and Social Media, Cambridge, MA: MIT Press.

Ruppert, Evelyn (2013): "Rethinking Empirical Social Sciences." In: Dialogues in Human Geography 3/3, pp. 268–73.

Ruppert, Evelyn/Law, John/Savage, Mike (2013): "Rethinking Empirical Social Sciences." In: Theory, Culture & Society 30/4, pp. 22–46.

Simondon, Gilbert (1958): Du mode d'existence des objets techniques, Paris: Aubier.

Stiegler, Bernard (1998): Technics and Time 1: The Fault of Epimetheus, Stanford: Stanford University Press.

Stiegler, Bernard (2010): Technics and Time 3: Cinematic Time and the Question of Malaise, Stanford: Stanford University Press.

Wark, McKenzie (2005): A Hacker Manifesto, Cambridge, MA: Harvard University Press.

Whitson, Gordon (2011): "How to Block Ads in Android Browsers and Apps." In: Lifehacker (http://lifehacker.com/5851038/how-to-block-ads-in-android-browsers-and-apps).

Digital Methodologies

From Data Analytics to Data Hermeneutics
Online Political Discussions, Digital Methods and the Continuing Relevance of Interpretive Approaches

Paolo Gerbaudo

Abstract

To advance the study of digital politics it is urgent to complement data analytics *with* data hermeneutics *to be understood as a methodological approach that focuses on the interpretation of the deep structures of meaning in social media conversations as they develop around various political phenomena, from digital protest movements to online election campaigns. The diffusion of Big Data techniques in recent scholarship on political behavior has led to a quantitative bias in the understanding of online political phenomena and a disregard for issues of content and meaning. To solve this problem it is necessary to adapt the hermeneutic approach to the conditions of social media communication, and shift its object of analysis from texts to datasets. On the one hand, this involves identifying procedures to select samples of social media posts out of datasets, so that they can be analysed in more depth. I describe three sampling strategies – top sampling, random sampling and zoom-in sampling – to attain this goal. On the other hand, "close reading" procedures used in hermeneutic analysis need to be adapted to the different quality of digital objects vis-à-vis traditional texts. This can be achieved by analysing posts not only as data-points in a dataset, but also as interventions in a collective conversation, and as utterances of broader "discourses". The task of interpretation of social media data also requires an understanding of the political and social contexts in which digital political phenomena unfold, as well as taking into account the subjective viewpoints and motivations of those involved, which can be gained through in-depth interviews, and other qualitative social science methods. Data hermeneutics thus holds promise for a closing of the gap between quantitative and qualitative approaches in the study of digital politics, allowing for a deeper and more holistic understanding of online political phenomena.*

Keywords: Big data; digital politics; hermeneutics; data analytics qualitative methods; random sampling; close reading.

Introduction

The digital transformation of our societies has not just transformed the "ontology" of politics, i.e. the nature or essence of contemporary political phenomena in a variety of domains, from social movements using data leaks as protest tactics to political campaigns mastering the art of data-driven targeted advertising. It has also transformed the "epistemology" of political research, i.e. the methods used to analyse political phenomena as they unfold online. If opinion surveys, statistical studies of electoral behaviour, content analysis of political speeches and news broadcasts have long been the tools of the trade for political analysts, we are now witnessing the development of an array of digital methods in political research – sophisticated computational techniques that are employed to sift the ocean of information contemporary politics is immersed in.

The most popular method in the emerging field of digital politics – the fledgling field of scholarship that explores the variety of political phenomena enabled by digital technology – is undoubtedly data analytics. Data analytics can be described as a series of techniques for statistical and computational analysis of various types of digital datasets (Kambatka 2014). Social scientists have used various kinds of econometric tools to analyse the different aspects of social media conversations, typically including: their network structure (see for example, González-Bailón et al. 2013); the temporal evolution of conversations (Conover et al. 2013); the process of information diffusion (Theocharis 2013); and the correlation of various popularity metrics, such as the number of likes or retweets (Dubois et al 2014).

Data analytics has enriched research on digital politics, by providing sophisticated ways to study and visualise online political dynamics. However, it has fast become a sort of methodological orthodoxy in the field, leading some researchers to overlook its manifold limits and shortcomings (Tufecki 2014; boyd/Crawford 2014). More importantly, its quantitative bias has contributed to marginalizing questions of cultural meaning and social motivation, which are fundamental to understand the content of social media conversations (Couldry/Stephansen 2014).

This article aims at fleshing out an alternative, qualitative approach to the study of online political phenomena that addresses some of the problems with data analytics. This is what I term "data hermeneutics", an updating of the interpretive methods originating from a number of disciplines including phenomenological philosophy, literary criticism, qualitative sociology and cultural anthropology – to deal with the specific properties of digital communication and social media datasets. Political research cannot content itself with ever more sophisticated forms of computational analysis of political behavior online. It also needs to answer qualitative questions about the "who", "what", "how" and "why" of digital political phenomena. If it has to have any real explanatory power, it has to pay attention to the meaning and subjective viewpoints inherent in social media conversations and the contexts in which these conversations occur.

The tradition of hermeneutics with its focus on structures of deep meaning and subjective worldviews reflected by them, provides with an inspiring but outdated blueprint on how to pursue such endeavour. To make this approach current again it is necessary to revise it to match the peculiar conditions of digital communication, which has a non-linear, dialogic, extemporaneous, and interactive character. Whereas traditional hermeneutics has dealt with the analysis of various traditional "texts" (novels, films, political speeches, news articles), data hermeneutics needs to find ways to analyse online content, approaching data as "inscriptions" (Ricoeur 1971) or recorded traces of a peculiar form of social text: social media conversations.

I discuss two practical aspects of this digital adaptation of hermeneutics: 1) the development of qualitative sampling procedures geared at reducing the size of social media datasets; 2) the development of "close data reading" procedures that may help interpret in the context of larger conversations and in relation to a number of connected discourses, narratives, motivations and worldviews.

First, data hermeneutics requires sampling procedures aimed at reducing the size of the datasets to a scale amenable to qualitative analysis. I discuss three such procedures: top sampling, random sampling and zoom-in sampling. In the first case the database is filtered for the top messages based on a number of popularity metrics, such as number of retweets or of likes. In the second case the sample is obtained by selecting a random set of posts, (tweets or Facebook posts), which can be considered representative of a conversation. In the third case, the researcher zooms in on a particular point in the conversation deemed to be particularly significant – for example a spike in user engagement. These three procedures, which can be used in combination, provide researchers with a "select social media dataset" that can then be analysed in more depth.

Second, "close reading" and "in-depth analysis", expressions that condense the *modus operandi* of hermeneutics, need to be revised to match the properties of social media data vis-à-vis traditional texts. I propose a three-step "close data reading" procedure: reading posts as rows in a dataset; as part of the conversation; as part of a certain social discourse. First, the researcher reads posts as datapoints in a dataset, paying attention to specific content and stylistics of a given post. Second, she approaches posts as exchanges in the conversation they were "scraped" from, paying attention to their embeddedness in a dialogic communication. Third, a full understanding of the meaning of social media posts and conversations requires interpreting their themes in light of the cultural, social and political contexts they navigate. To this end researchers need to take into account the subjective viewpoints and motivations of participants, by using more traditional qualitative methodologies, such as in-depth interviews.

The article begins by reviewing the current debate on digital methods in digital politics research, focusing on a number of critical issues, and in particular the neglect for issues of meaning. The second part of the article moves instead to flesh out in the positive the data hermeneutics approach, by presenting connected sampling procedures and analytical techniques. The conclusion sums up the content of my methodological proposal and considers some of the questions and challenges ahead for digital politics research.

Beyond the quantitative bias of data analytics

Methodology in the emerging field of digital politics is dominated by "data analytics" (Kampatka et al. 2014), a set of statistical and computational techniques for the analysis of large social media datasets. The development of data analytics has been led by major internet firms as Facebook, Amazon and Twitter, which in recent years have created data science teams to develop sophisticated market intelligence (Chen et al. 2012). Social scientists, and more specifically political researchers, have been fast to follow this trend, using data analytics to study what happens in social media conversations, relevant to various political phenomena, from social movements to electoral campaigns and political debates (Theocharis 2013; González-Bailón et al. 2013; Conover et al., 2013). Data obtained by "mining" from the APIs of social network sites is subject to various forms of statistical and computational analysis. Among the most typical issues analysed via data analytics feature the structure of social media conversations often pictured through network diagrams; their clustering into distinct groupings sharing common features; the distribution and correlation between different social media metrics (followers, likes, shares, retweets etc.); the temporal evolution of conversations (peaks, lows, etc.); the frequency of key terms used in conversations.

Data analytics has provided innovative and sophisticated techniques to renew and advance sociological methods, beyond the current crisis of empirical sociology (Burrows/Savage 2007). It can be understood as a necessary update to traditional quantitative social science data such as surveys (Kitchin, 2014; Tinati, et al. 2014), facing up to the new methodological challenges posed by the abundance of social media data, and allowing to explore new social and political phenomena that have evident interest for research. Furthermore, data analytics offers great advancements the detail and sophistication of quantitative analysis, allowing researchers to conduct studies "at scale" (Kambatla 2014), examining the entire "population" of a given phenomenon or a close approximation.

These positive elements notwithstanding, data analytics has demonstrated significant shortcomings, which call for the development of alternative approaches. After an initial phase of naïve enthusiasm, in fact in recent years this methodological approach has begun to be criticized by a number of scholars, who have highlighted how data analytics frequently falls short of the standards expected in quantitative research (Tufekci 2014; Tinati et al. 2014; Lazer et al. 2013). Zeynep Tufekci has argued that in many circumstances there has been a "lack of clarity with regard to sampling, universe and representativeness" (Tufekci 2014: 324). Similarly Kate Crawford and danah boyd have highlighted that "claims to objectivity and accuracy are often misleading" and that it is erroneous to think that "bigger data is always better data" (2014: 217).

There is however a more fundamental critique that can be made against data analytics: its quantitative bias and its neglect of issues of meaning. By focusing on the mathematical *form* of social media conversations – its structure and dynamics – data analytics tends to overlook their *content*, and the deep meaning structures expressed in them and the motivations they betoken. Data analytics can reveal with great sophistication the mathematical properties of datasets, but it is not well equipped to answer qualitative questions about the "what", the "how" and the "why" of social media conversations. Also when content is analysed, as in computer-assisted textual analysis (Grimmer/Stewart 2013), the logic remains one of "counting occurrences", for example measuring frequency of certain terms, or the emotional tone of a conversation. This quantitative bias is exacerbated by the fact that data analytics-driven politics research often lacks in context (Tufekci 2014; Crawford/boyd 2014). To quote Clifford Geertz sometimes it is as if data analytics researchers seem to think that it is possible to understand phenomena without *knowing* then (1957: 64).

Looking at social media data as texts

The shortcomings of data analytics should be seen by qualitative researchers as evidence for the continuing relevance of interpretive methods. Social media data is not inherently hostile to a qualitative research agenda, and potentially offers a treasure trove for qualitative research. The abundant and fine-grained information that can be retrieved from online conversations, including textual information, pictures, videos, and other digital objects is a resource that waits to be tapped from a qualitative angle. Indeed some qualitative researchers have begun working in this direction, as seen in the field of online discourse analysis (Androutsopoulos/Beißwenger 2008; Kelsey/Bennett 2014). Yet, much still remains to be done in devising effective strategies and procedures for the analysis of social media data that can make qualitative methods relevant once again.

Data hermeneutics is a notion that proposes a radically different orientation from the one pursued by data analytics, by giving a new lease of life to one of the most old-fashioned of interpretive methods: the hermeneutic approach. Where data analytics operates according to a purely objectivist view of online political conversations, conceived of as forms of collective behaviour which can be objectively measured, data hermeneutics – alike all interpretive methodologies – operates with the idea that these conversations are first and foremost symbolic interactions which cannot be understood without taking into account the subjective viewpoints of those involved. Where data analytics – as in fact all forms of analytics – involves various forms of numerical analysis, drawn from the field of statistics and computation, data hermeneutics centers on the symbolic analysis of the meaning structures of online conversations, in light of connected social discourses and motivations. Finally, where – as the very etymology of the term analytics suggests – data analytics is mostly interested in *analyzing* that is in "breaking down" a given phenomenon into basic units and variables for statistical analysis, data hermeneutics' chief concern is the synthetic aim of interpreting, reconstructing and explaining the overarching narratives that underpin social media conversations.

Data hermeneutics is a digital adaptation of hermeneutics, a term that derives from the ancient Greek word "hermeneuo" which means to "understand" or to "interpret" and can be described as a broadly developed set of methodologies for interpretation (Szondi 1975). The origins of this approach hark back to Greek antiquity and medieval philosophy, with its interest in the different literal and allegorical layer of meaning of sacred texts. In modern times hermeneutics has been associated with phenomenological philosophy, and in particular the work of Edmund Husserl (1970), Martin Heidegger and his pupil Hans Georg Gadamer (2004), and has influenced a wide array of social and political theorists, including Max Weber (1978; 1981), Walter Benjamin (1977), Fredric Jameson (1981) and Anthony Giddens (1984). The hermeneutic interpretive approach has also profoundly shaped research methods in the humanities and social sciences, as most evidently seen in the context of new criticism, qualitative sociology and social anthropology (Bleicher/Bleicher 1980).

In the context of literary criticism (Bressler 1999), hermeneutic approaches have informed the development of "close reading" procedures (Wolfreys 2000). Close reading can be described as a process of deep analytical engagement with a text – a novel, a poem, but also a film or any other similar artefact – with the aim of exploring the complex network of meaning that underpins it. Thus, for example, in analyzing a novel, a film, or a political speech, literary scholars look at their content and formal characteristics, such as the language, tone, imagery, and rhetorical figures. While sometimes – as in the case of New Criticism and semiotics – this analysis can take an purely formalistic character, close reading has also been used in the context of more sociologically minded discourse analysis approaches, as performed for example in the context of cultural studies and sociology (Wodak/Krzyzanowski 2008), looking for the connection between specific texts and broader discourses.

In social science, the hermeneutic approach has been popular among both sociologists and anthropologists. Key in this respect has been Max Weber's view of sociology as an interpretive science, different from the natural sciences, because the subjects and objects of analysis are both human beings, bestowed with consciousness and reflexivity (Tucker 1965). The priority for the social sciences, vis-à-vis the natural sciences, is *Verstehen*, the in-depth understanding of the subjective viewpoints, motives and worldviews that inform social action, rather than action as just an externally observable behaviour (Weber 1978; 1981). Anthony Giddens expanded on this idea by coining the notion of "double hermeneutics", which highlight how social science studies does not study only people's behaviour but also people's interpretation of the social world and of their social action, and thus revolves around an interpretation of already existing interpretations, or the scholarly interpretation of lay conceptions (1984: 20).

The hermeneutic approach has also been taken up by social anthropologists such as Clifford Geertz, who argued that in producing "thick descriptions" of communities and social practices, anthropologists should take into account "the interpretations to which persons of a particular denomination subject their experience" (1973: 15). He argued that interpretive methods required an effort to "find one's feet" (Geertz 1973: 18) in the phenomena, or to use another metaphor "put oneself in the shoes" of the actors and communities analysed, looking at people as conscious and creative subjects rather than objects prey to social forces they cannot control. This interpretive orientation has been at the heart of qualitative methods such as in-depth interviews and focus groups and has informed the development of the now popular "grounded theory" approach (Strauss/Corbyn 1998) in which researchers are expected to develop their interpretation of social phenomena in a bottom-up manner, rather than testing a-priori hypotheses.

In recent years there have been some inklings of a digital adaptation of hermeneutics, as signaled by terms as "computational hermeneutics" (Harnad 1990; Mohr et al. 2013) and "digital hermeneutics" (Capurro 2000). Rafael Capurro for example has argued that hermeneutics needs to face up to the challenge of digital technology, and develop an "understanding [of] the foundations of digital technology and its interplay with human existence" (ibid: 37). This article contributes to this emerging line of methodological reflection and practice, by exploring specific strategies and procedures for the specific purpose of social media analysis and digital politics research.

A digital adaptation of hermeneutics, does not simply entail saying that hermeneutics needs to "find its own feet" in the digital world, but also that to understand the digital world it is necessary to recuperate the concern with interpretation which is ultimately hermeneutics' *raison d'être*. This assertion is a highly contentious one, due to the anti-interpretive character of the ideology of Big Data, or "dataism" (Van Dijck 2014) – and the idea that data is already a ready-made form of knowledge which does not require active interpretation. This persuasion has been put forward most explicitly in a famous article by *Wired* magazine editor Chris Anderson, where he argued that in the present data deluge "[c]orrelation is enough. We can stop looking for models. We can analyze the data without hypotheses about what it might show" (2008). This intervention has been criticized as going too far by other Big data experts (Bollier/Firestone 2010; Cukier/Mayer-Schönberger 2013: 72). Yet, it is interesting precisely because it reveals in condensed form the overly positivist and anti-hermeneutic stance of data science.

Anderson's prophecy about the end of theory and interpretation neglects a number of facts. First, there is no such a thing as "raw data", which is in fact an "oxymoron" (Gitelman 2013), since data is always structured in higher order categories that reflect various biases and assumptions as expressed in the DIKW (Data, Information, Knowledge, Wisdom) hierarchy used in Informatics (Rowley 2007). Secondly, datasets display a number of social and political biases that reflect and sometimes amplify social inequality (O'Neil 2016), and can be identified only through processes of in-depth interpretation. Thirdly, the overabundance of data makes the task of interpretation particularly important. As argued by Alyssa Wise and David Shaffer "with larger amounts of data, theory plays an ever-more critical role in analysis" (2015: 5). Therefore, rather than hastily throwing interpretation out of the window, it is urgent to revive and revise interpretive methodologies to match the conditions of a digital era.

The main challenge data hermeneutics is to shift from texts to data as the main object of analysis; or better to find ways to read data as text, that is as a partly coherent and discrete web of meaning. Interpretive approaches have traditionally been concerned with analyzing texts – novels, poems, films, speeches, interviews, field-notes, etc. – by examining them in great depth sentence by sentence, one might say, or even word by word, as signified by notions as "close reading" and "in-depth analysis" frequently referred to as methodological short-hands. Social media conversations may indeed analysed in ways similar to the analysis of traditional texts, such as by exploring their language, imagery, tone, and other stylistics. However, significant modifications are necessary due the specific nature of social media as objects of analysis.

With their non-linear, extemporaneous, and interactive nature, social media conversations are radically different from a novel, a film, or an ethnographic field-note. Consider for example the way in which social media resemble more oral conversations, rather than written texts; the way in which each tweet or Facebook message can hardly be understood in isolation from other messages; the sheer quantity of social media messages and the connected risk of information overload; the speed and instantaneity of conversations; their fluid and networked character; or the way in which the various interactions available on social media (such as liking, retweeting, or favouriting) add another layer of meaning that was unknown in pre-digital texts (Van Dijck/Poell 2013). These idiosyncrasies of online communication pose serious challenge to interpretive approaches and require significant adaptations. In the continuation of this article I focus on two practical issues relevant in the development of data hermeneutics: a) "small data" sampling methods; b) and "close data reading" procedures.

Sampling social media datasets for qualitative analysis

The main obstacle for data hermeneutics lies precisely in the "Big-ness" of Big Data, in the vastness of datasets available to researchers. While this is the aspect that makes social media datasets so interesting for quantitative researchers due to their great level of detail and the possibility to study conversations "at scale", it is also the element which is most problematic for qualitative researchers who are used instead to work with "small data" (Couldry/Stephasen 2014). Qualitative researchers are expected to engage at length with research material, exploring the fine-grained meaning structure of texts and connected discourses. This approach limits the amount of evidence which can be analysed. The employment of textual analysis software such as NVivo or ATLAS.ti (Friese 2014), provides only partial solace. Ultimately effective close reading continues to imply a great deal of "manual" coding by "human operators". From this situation it follows that the main challenge for data hermeneutics is one of focus: reducing the amount of data to analyse, to a selected sample which can still be considered significant and representative of a given aspect of the conversation.

Three sampling procedures can be used to perform this task: top sampling, random sampling, and zoom-in sampling. First, one may decide to sample for top, by focusing on the messages which – based on a number of popularity metrics (likes, retweets, shares) – can be considered as the most visible or important in a given conversation. Second, a different strategy involves random sampling, selecting by chance a subset of messages from a given conversation using appropriate software. Third, "zoom-in sampling" involves concentrating on a particular period of time in the conversation, which for whatever reason is considered particularly significant (start dates of protest waves, election days, etc.). Each of these sampling procedures provides a different approximation to a data sample for qualitative analysis, and will therefore befit different research questions and designs.

Top sampling is a strategy that has already been utilised by researchers, especially those interested in the behaviour of "power users", user that have disproportionate level of influence on online conversations (Cha et al. 2010), on the basis of a number of popularity metrics (likes, retweets, favourites etc.) Practically, sampling at the top is fairly easy and can be performed by using standard spreadsheet software such as Microsoft Excel, selecting the column of the variable one takes as the most indicative of the popularity of messages, ordering in descending order, and then filtering the top 50, 100, 200, 1000 messages. The viewpoint over a conversation offered by this procedure is evidently biased. It only affords an understanding of what happens "at the top" of a conversation and its most influential users and messages. This procedure is particularly suitable when it comes to highly public and visible conversations which tend to have a strong power law distribution and few communication centres (Gonzalez-Bailon et al. 2011; 2013). However, it is less desirable when analysing less topical conversations, and cannot be considered representative of the average of a given conversation. It is good to look at the peak of conversations, not to explore explore the "base".

The second sampling procedures is random sampling. Random sampling is an already well-rehashed sampling strategy in the social sciences (Patton 2005) which involves selecting by chance a sub-set of a given population. This approach can be updated in a digital context by using a number of digital tools such as T-CAT tool developed by the Digital Methods Initiative (DMI) at the University of

Amsterdam. This type of sampling strategy has many advantages. It can return a sample that can be considered representative of the totality of messages contained in a given dataset. As it is the case with random sampling more generally, the representativeness of the sample depends on the ratio between the size of the population analysed and the size of the dataset: the greater the ration, the greater the risk the sample may not be truly representative (Marshall 1996). This approach can be used if one is interested in getting a general sense of the type of messages to be found at the "base" of a conversation, including messages with relatively low popularity.

The third sampling strategy is zoom-in or peak sampling, a sampling procedure that focuses on a given time in the conversation that is of particular interest to the researcher. These may include online reflections of "real world" events (a protest event, or an election) or moments of high user engagement on social media, or any other event considered of particular significance to understand the dynamics of the conversation. In my own research I adopted this strategy to look at the online preparation of major protest events in the Arab Spring and the Indignados, where one could see the build-up of "digital enthusiasm" (Gerbaudo 2016). The advantage of zoom-in sampling is that it concentrates on moments that can be particularly revealing of a number of digital political dynamics, such as the nexus between social media and mobilization, or the social media reflection of offline events. Its main disadvantage is obviously its temporally limited coverage, and the fact that it thus returns a selective image of the conversation.

These three sampling procedures may be used in combination in the design of concrete research projects. For example, if one is interested in the way in which key top social media accounts reacted to a certain incident, zoom-in sampling and top sampling may be utilized in concert. The combination of two or more sampling procedures can also help more easily achieve the aim of "dataset reduction" which – as we have previously seen – is a condition of possibility for data hermeneutics. As a rule of a thumb, based on my own experience conducting various digital politics research projects, when sampling from large datasets researchers should aim for a dataset numbering between 1000 and 100,000 words, which roughly equates between 40 and 4,000 tweets. This corpus is comparable in size to the ones traditionally studied by qualitative researchers – novels, films, political speeches, and the like – and small enough to be analysed in-depth by a "human operator" without falling prey to information overload.

Data close reading

Besides reducing the size of datasets, data hermeneutics entails a rethinking of the procedures traditionally used to analyse texts, for the purpose of adapting them to social media data analysis. This is what can be described as "close reading of data" or "data close reading", an adaptation of close reading procedures to the specific conditions of social media communication. Hermeneutic researchers in the humanities and social sciences have typically studied texts, where the notion of text is not limited to written texts, but to all compositions, artworks, and social performances that can be understood as relatively discrete and coherent symbolic objects. In the case of literary criticism, typical texts have included novels, poems and films; in the social sciences, everyday behaviour, public performances and similar phenomena cam also be read as texts, often by producing textual accounts of them, such as ethnographic field-notes. In approaching these texts qualitative researchers have typically aimed for an in-depth engagement with the object of analysis. This stance is most clearly revealed by the term "close reading" used in literary criticism, which highlights how researchers are expected to explore texts in great detail, deciphering their complex and largely invisible deep meaning structures, and their connection to broader narratives and discourses.

The analytical process in qualitative research typically involves the use of various "coding" procedures whereby the researcher marks out certain portion of text as belonging to certain overarching themes, which can then be organized in broader categories and narratives. As argued by Johnny Saldana, a code in this context can be described as "a word or short phrase that symbolically assigns a summative, salient, essence-capturing, or evocative attribute for a portion of language-based or visual data" (2015: 4). This methodology has been applied to such diverse types of data as interviews, ethnographic observations, films, and newspaper articles. It is easy to understand how such approach can be used to analyse traditional texts, or social events and rituals that are relatively circumscribed, coherent and mostly linear in their form. But how does close reading functions when studying social media data?

Close data reading needs to approach social media data as "texts", considering data-points, e.g. Facebook posts or tweets, as meaningful messages. Reflecting back on my experience conducting digital politics research I propose that close data reading should proceed in different steps, allowing to progressively "close in" on the deep meaning structures of posts and conversations. Selected social media datasets, obtained through the sampling procedures previously described, can be analysed in three steps which all imply a different "gaze" on research data: reading posts as rows in a dataset; as part of the conversation; as part of a certain social discourse.

First, Facebook posts and Twitter posts can be read as rows in a dataset, the practical form in which they manifest themselves to qualitative researchers at the start of a project. Researchers typically view such datasets in the form of a long table of rows, to be browsed through via spreadsheet software or via qualitative analysis software such as NVivo or ATLAS.ti. Thereby posts appear in their rawest form as mere rows listed in a table, chunks of interactions now stripped from their surrounding context of a live conversation, and which now appears in the dead form of data-points. A number of elements can however already be identified at this stage. Researchers can explore the topics discussed in each post, as well as the form they are expressed in, such as the use of a certain type of language, imagery, tone, or specific rhetorical figures. In the case of my own research on the 2011 protest movements, this step of analysis already allowed to identify a number of significant features of online protest discourse including: the use of a conversational and exhortative language (2016); the popularity of different memes (2015); the adoption of the entire gamut of typical social media tropes from emoticons, to sloganeering shortened sentences; and in terms of content the abundance of reference to unifying subjects, as "the people", the citizenry, or the 99 % (2014).

The second level of analysis involves repositioning posts in their original environment, reading them in the "live" context of the conversations. This step approaches social media data as the traces or inscriptions of a specific type of social text: a social media conversation. Yet, to better understand the meaning of posts it is necessary to approach these data-points not as texts in and of themselves, but rather as traces or "inscription" (Ricoeur 1972), that is the partial and largely arbitrary recordings of live social media conversations. To get a sense of how a message was perceived by internet users it is necessary to read it in the context of the conversations in which it was uttered. Practically, this can be done by browsing the associated web address and exploring the conversations it contributed to. It is useful for this purpose to create a folder of screenshots of conversations, one can then refer back to during the analysis. In my research, this step of analysis helped me to understand the intense emotional dialogue developed in such movements as the Egyptian 2011 uprising and the Spanish Indignados, and the way users reinforced positive messages channeled by activist social media, thus fuelling a wave of "digital enthusiasm" (2016). By reading posts in their lived contexts, we can understand the degree to which they are in-tune with the mood of internet communities, and the content of the dialogic discourse that emerges out social media interactions.

The third step for the close reading of data – the one which is more similar to traditional coding procedures – explores the discourses and deeper structures of meaning of a given post. Like with step two, the gist is to avoid reading posts in isolation. However, in this case the connections one needs to pay attention to are not just the ones with other messages within a specific conversation, but the links between the message and broader discourses that act as background and source of meaning for a given message. Important to this end is that researchers acquired an understanding of the context in which digital political phenomena operate and the subjective motives of participants as it can be secured by tapping into more traditional qualitative methods. In the case of my own research the most important traditional methods used in tandem with data hermeneutics were in-depth interviews with protest movement participants active on social media which allowed to gain an in-depth understanding of their subjective viewpoints and backgrounds. Further contextual sources of information that can aid interpretation include ethnographic observation, archival documents, and similar sources of background information about a given phenomenon.

A practical example of how this cultural understanding can aid the work of social media interpretation can be offered considering the famous "Bring tent" tweet by the Canadian countercultural magazine *Adbusters* that first launched the Occupy Wall Street movement. In and of itself this tweet seems to have quite limited meaning, too short and cryptic to allow for analysis. Yet, seen in the cultural context of contemporary social movements, of post-modern neo-anarchism and of a nascent Occupy Wall Street movement, some interesting elements can be inferred from it. For someone who knows the context of this tweet, the nature, motivations and aims of the Occupy movement, the message resonates for a number of motives, including the appeal to participate in the Occupy movement; the action format of the occupation; the pragmatism of the movement; its distrust in traditional ideologies, and its connected emphasis on the political significance of concrete and practical activities, such as the act of bringing a tent and setting it up in a protest camp in a central public space.

This three-step of analysis allow researchers to move deeper and deeper in the web of meanings of social media conversations. At each step the research progressively "closes in" on the interpretation of posts and social media conversations, while at the same time broadening the perspective of analysis, and paying attention to the general context. This procedure is evidently not an exact science. To quote Clifford Geertz is more of an artisanal process of "guessing at meanings, assessing the guesses, and drawing explanatory conclusions from the better guesses" (1973: 20). Researchers should verify the validity of their emerging interpretation of meanings, by "triangulating", that is comparing and contrasting the findings emerging from different posts, and progressively refining their interpretation.

Conclusion

As I have sought to demonstrate in this article, a digital update of the hermeneutic method – data hermeneutics – is urgently needed to overcome the limits of data analytics. Crunching numbers in ever more powerful and sophisticated ways is not enough, if one is not able to fully explain the categories of analysis, and the significance, ramifications, and implications of findings. While "counting" – the core logic of data analytics – can no doubt be useful in gaining an overview of the structure and dynamics of conversations, a real understanding of their motivations and meanings can be achieved through the sampling and close reading procedures proposed in this article. To make sense of online political phenomena, we cannot approach them as merely structures of behaviour to be studied mathematically. We also need to approach them as texts, webs of meanings which researchers need to slowly acquaint themselves with before they can claim to know them and comprehend them. Research based on data metrics has been weak in depth of understanding and contextual knowledge, and it is precisely in these areas that data hermeneutics can give a timely contribution.

The idea of data hermeneutics put forward in this article is in part a polemical response to the current dominance of data analytics in social science, and a reassertion of the importance of qualitative methods. However, when it comes to designing concrete research projects, data hermeneutics should be understood as non-exclusive. Data analytics and data hermeneutics should often be used in tandem, as part of a "quanti-qualitative" approach (Venturini/Latour 2008), with various iterations between the two. Data analytics is particularly precious in the initial scoping of a research project, since it allows to gain an overview of conversation structures, from which researchers can then turn towards data hermeneutics, looking in more depth at the content of specific messages, and specific excerpts of a given conversation. Data hermeneutics can improve on quantitative approaches by providing a clearer understanding of various categories utilized in such analyses. For example in analyzing the language utilized in a given conversation one can combine qualitative and quantitative methods in effective ways, by identifying the most recurrent terms and then looking at how these terms are concretely used in a number of expressions, and finally investigating the motivations underlying these expressions. Furthermore, statistical testing procedures from data analytics can provide indications on where to go deeper, for example by highlighting the peaks of activity in a certain dataset and thus suggesting where a more in-depth quantitative analysis should be conducted.

Thus, what is required is not the wholesale substitution of data analytics with data hermeneutics, but a methodological rebalancing the ultimately can benefit both qualitative and quantitative research, and more generally allow for a more holistic and better contextualized understanding of contemporary politics.

References

Anderson, Chris (2008): "The end of theory: The data deluge makes the scientific method obsolete." In: Wired magazine 16/7 (https://www.wired.com/2008/06/pb-theory/).

Androutsopoulos, Jannis/Beißwenger, Michael (2008): "Introduction: Data and methods in computer-mediated discourse analysis." In: Language@Internet 5/2, pp. 1–7.

Batrinca, Bogdan/Treleaven, Philip C. (2015): "Social media analytics: a survey of techniques, tools and platforms." In: AI & Society, 30/1, pp. 89–116.

Benjamin, Walter (1977): The origin of German tragic drama, London: NLB.

Bleicher, Josef (1980): Contemporary hermeneutics: Hermeneutics as method, philosophy and critique, London: Routledge & Kegan Paul.

Bollier, David/Firestone, Charles M. (2010): The promise and peril of big data, Washington, DC: Aspen Institute.

boyd, dana/Crawford, Kate (2012): "Critical questions for big data: Provocations for a cultural, technological, and scholarly phenomenon." In: Information, Communication & Society 15/5, pp. 662–679.

Bressler, Charles E. (1999): Literary criticism: An introduction to theory and practice, Upper Saddle River, NJ: Prentice Hall.

Burrows, Roger/Savage, Michael (2007): "The coming crisis of empirical sociology." In: Sociology 41/5, pp. 885–899.

Capurro, Robert (2010): "Digital hermeneutics: An outline." In: AI & Society 25/1, pp. 35–42.

Cha, Meyung/Haddadi, Hamed/Benevenuto, Fabricio/Gummadi, P. Krishna (2010): "Measuring User Influence in Twitter: The Million Follower Fallacy." In: ICWSM 10/30, pp. 10–17.

Chen, Hsinchun/Chiang, Roger H./Storey, Veda C. (2012): "Business Intelligence and Analytics: From Big Data to Big Impact." In: MIS Quarterly 36/4, pp. 1165–1188.

Conover, Michael D./Ferrara, Emilio/Menczer, Filippo/Flammini, Alessandro (2013): "The digital evolution of occupy wall street." In: PloS one 8/5.

Dubois, Elizabeth/Gaffney, Devin (2014): "The multiple facets of influence: Identifying political influentials and opinion leaders on Twitter." In: American Behavioral Scientist 58/10, pp. 1260–1277.

Friese, Susanne (2014): Qualitative data analysis with ATLAS.ti, London: Sage.

Gadamer, Hans-Georg (2004): Truth and Method, New York: Bloomsbury Publishing.

Giddens, Anthony (1984): The constitution of society: Outline of the theory of structuration, Berkeley: University of California Press.

Gerbaudo, Paolo (2012): Tweets and the streets: Social media and contemporary activism, London: Pluto Press.

Gerbaudo, P. (2014): "The 'Movements of the Squares' and the Contested Resurgence of the 'Sovereign People' in Contemporary Protest Culture". In: SSRN 2439359.

Gerbaudo, Paolo (2015): "Protest avatars as memetic signifiers: political profile pictures and the construction of collective identity on social media in the 2011 protest wave." In: Information, Communication & Society 18/8, pp. 916–929.

Gerbaudo, Paolo (2016): "Rousing the Facebook Crowd: Digital Enthusiasm and Emotional Contagion in the 2011 Protests in Egypt and Spain." In: International Journal of Communication 10/20, pp. 254–273.

Gibbs, Graham R. (2002): Qualitative data analysis: Explorations with NVivo, Buckingham: Open University Press.

Gitelman, Lisa (2013): "Raw data" is an Oxymoron, Cambridge, MA: MIT Press.

González-Bailón, Sandra/Borge-Holthoefer, Javier/Rivero, Alejandro/Moreno, Yamir (2011): "The dynamics of protest recruitment through an online network." In: Scientific Reports 1/197.

González-Bailón, Sandra/Borge-Holthoefer, Javier/Moreno, Yamir (2013): "Broadcasters and hidden influentials in online protest diffusion." In: American Behavioral Scientist 57/7, pp. 920–942.

Grimmer, Justin/Stewart, Brandon M. (2013): "Text as data: The promise and pitfalls of automatic content analysis methods for political texts." In: Political Analysis 21/3, pp. 267–297.

Harnad, Stevan (1990): "Against computational hermeneutics." In: Social Epistemology 4, pp. 167–172.

Husserl, Edmund (1970): The crisis of European sciences and transcendental phenomenology: An introduction to phenomenological philosophy, Evanston: Northwestern University Press.

Jameson, Fredric (1981): The political unconscious: literature as a socially symbolic act, London: Methuen.

Kelsey, Darren/Bennett, Lucy (2014): "Discipline and resistance on social media: Discourse, power and context in the Paul Chambers 'Twitter Joke Trial'." In: Discourse, Context & Media 3, pp. 37–45.

Kitchin, Robert (2014): The data revolution: Big data, open data, data infrastructures and their consequences, London: Sage.

Lazer, David/Kennedy, Ryan/King, Gary/Vespignani, Alessandro (2014): "The parable of Google Flu: traps in big data analysis." In: Science 343/6176, pp. 1203–1205.

Marshall, Martin N. (1996): "Sampling for qualitative research." In: Family practice 13/6, pp. 522–526.

O'Neil, Cathy (2016): Weapons of math destruction: How big data increases inequality and threatens democracy, New York: Crown.

Patton, Michael Quinn (2005): Qualitative research, Chichester: John Wiley & Sons.

Ricoeur, Paul (1971): "The model of the text: Meaningful action considered as a text." In: Social research 38, pp. 529–562.

Rogers, Richard (2013): Digital methods, Cambridge, MA: MIT Press.

Rowley, Jennifer E. (2007): "The wisdom hierarchy: representations of the DIKW hierarchy." In: Journal of Information Science, 33/2, pp. 163–180.

Saldaña, John (2015): The coding manual for qualitative researchers, London: Sage.

Stephansen, Hilde C./Couldry, Nick (2014): "Understanding micro-processes of community building and mutual learning on Twitter: A 'small data' approach." In: Information, Communication & Society 17/10, pp. 1212–1227.

Strauss, Anselm/Corbin, Juliet (1990): Basics of qualitative research, Newbury Park, CA: Sage.

Theocharis, Yannis (2013): "The wealth of (occupation) networks? Communication patterns and information distribution in a Twitter protest network." In: Journal of Information Technology & Politics 10/1, pp. 35–56.

Tinati, Ramine/Halford, Susan/Carr, Leslie/Pope, Catherine (2014): "Big data: methodological challenges and approaches for sociological analysis." In: Sociology, 0038038513511561.
Tucker, William T. (1965): "Max Weber's 'Verstehen'." In: The Sociological Quarterly 6/2, pp. 157–165.
Tufekci, Zeynep (2014): "Big questions for social media big data: Representativeness, validity and other methodological pitfalls." In: arXiv, 1403.7400.
van Dijck, José (2014): "Datafication, dataism and dataveillance: Big Data between scientific paradigm and ideology." In: Surveillance & Society 12/2.
Venturini, Tommaso/Latour, Bruno (2010): "The social fabric: Digital traces and quali-quantitative methods." In: Proceedings of Future En Seine 2009, pp. 87–101.
Weber, Max (1978): Economy and society: An outline of interpretive sociology, Berkeley: University of California Press.
Weber, Max (1981): "Some Categories of Interpretive Sociology." In: The Sociological Quarterly 22/2, pp. 151–180.
Wise, Alyssa F./Shaffer, David W. (2015): "Why theory matters more than ever in the age of big data." In: Journal of Learning Analytics 2/2, pp. 5–13.
Wodak, Ruth/Krzyzanowski, Michal (2008): Qualitative discourse analysis in the Social Sciences, London: Palgrave Macmillan.
Wolfreys, Julian (2000): Readings: Acts of close reading in literary theory, Edinburgh: Edinburgh University Press.

Visual Social Media and Big Data
Interpreting Instagram Images Posted on Twitter

Dhiraj Murthy, Alexander Gross, Marisa McGarry

Abstract

Social media such as Twitter and Instagram are fast, free, and multicast. These attributes make them particularly useful for crisis communication. However, the speed and volume also make them challenging to study. Historically, journalists controlled what/how images represented crises. Large volumes of social media can change the politics of representing disasters. However, methodologically, it is challenging to study visual social media data. Specifically, the process is usually labour-intensive, using human coding of images to discern themes and subjects. For this reason, Studies investigating social media during crises tend to examine text. In addition, application programming interfaces (APIs) for visual social media services such as Instagram and Snapchat are restrictive or even non-existent. Our work uses images posted by Instagram users on Twitter during Hurricane Sandy as a case study. This particular case is unique as it is perhaps the first US disaster where Instagram played a key role in how victims experienced Sandy. It is also the last major US disaster to take place before Instagram images were removed from Twitter feeds. Our sample consists of 11,964 Instagram images embedded into tweets during a two-week timeline surrounding Hurricane Sandy. We found that the production and consumption of selfies, food/drink, pets, and humorous macro images highlight possible changes in the politics of representing disasters – a potential turn from top-down understandings of disasters to bottom-up, citizen informed views. Ultimately, we argue that image data produced during crises has potential value in helping us understand the social experience of disasters, but studying these types of data presents theoretical and methodological challenges.

Keywords: social media; Instagram; Twitter; image posting; crisis communication; humour; big data.

> "I expect that the number of photos uploaded to Facebook daily is larger than all artifacts stored in all the world's museums"
> LEV MANOVICH (2012: 461)

Introduction

Social media has become an important medium of communication during crises – from natural disasters to violent events such as shootings and terrorist events. In the case of the former, users producing and consuming content on social media help tell the story of what is happening on the ground from the vantage point of victims. These content can also serve to alert emergency services as to what victims are asking for. Social media can be used to both gauge public reactions as well as help track down perpetrators via citizen-based surveillance. In all these cases, big data methods are deployed, but they tend to leverage the analysis of text. Though the posting of images and video during crises has become an important part of how crises are socially experienced, methods to study not only the large volume of data being produced during crises, but the speed and complexity of them has perhaps discouraged some social researchers from studying visual social media.

Indeed, despite social media moving towards a state of including visual content as a norm, scholarship has been slow to grasp the methodological challenges of this change. This is partially attributable to the fact that 'social media are a moving target', creating challenges for identifying consistencies across platforms (Hogan/Quan-Haase 2010). In addition, visual social media platforms such a Snapchat and Instagram have restrictive or inaccessible application programming interfaces (APIs), the systems by which external users can directly access platform data. Closed or semi-closed APIs make it difficult to collect many types of visual social media data. Though these data can be immensely constructive to studies ranging from health (Seltzer et al. 2015) to disasters (Yates/Paquette 2011), a disproportionate amount of work is focused on criminal contexts, such as being able to identify people and places (Zhenguo et al. 2015) and deploy police or security services accordingly, what has sometimes been called 'predictive policing' (Lupton 2015, 100). In addition, the majority of work is largely quantitative and tends to rely on computerized visual recognition (e. g. Xinpeng et al. 2015, whose work seeks to automatically identify hackers through their social media profiles). Images produced and consumed during disasters likely perform multiple functions and such methods are generally unidimensional by definition.

To help bridge this gap, our study uses an empirical case study of 11,964 geolocated images taken by users of the popular mobile photo sharing app Instagram and posted on Twitter during Hurricane Sandy. Not only was the October 29, 2012 storm the most destructive in recent memory, but it is perhaps the first major US disaster where Instagram played a major role in how it was socially experienced. In addition, Sandy was the first and last major US disaster to take place when Instagram images were natively embedded within Twitter feeds, providing a unique case where images are networked across two major social media platforms.

Instagram pictures posted to Twitter are an uncommon case for several reasons. First, Twitter data are readily collectible and are well-known for having an open API that enables large volumes of data to be harvested (Murthy and Bowman 2014). Second, most social media platforms are walled off for commercial reasons. Instagram was still in its infancy and saw convergence with Twitter as a positive force. At the time of our study, an image taken with the Instagram application could be directly embedded into a user's tweet, making it fully accessible via Twitter's relatively open API. In December 2012, Instagram disabled this service and as of June, 2016, the platform shut off most third-party direct application access (Cook 2016). Our study of Hurricane Sandy is distinct both in its study of Instagram images posted on Twitter and its method of human coding nearly 12,000 images. The latter allows us to better understand Sandy through the eyes of its victims. Our study also seeks to understand the collective, and perhaps alternative, narratives that can be discerned through analysing this large volume of image data.

Background

Big data and visual social media

Big data has traditionally been defined through the 3Vs – variety, velocity, and volume (Kaisler et al. 2013). This initial framing was extended by Kitchin (2014: 1–2), who argued that big data are also "exhaustive in scope [,...] fine-grained in resolution [....,] relational in nature [... and] flexible". In other words, big data is not just about being big, but also signifies detail, precision, and unique abilities to correlate across very diverse variables. Simply put: "Bigger data are not always better data" (boyd/Crawford 2012: 668). And how we think about big data research methods also matters. Ruppert (2015) argues that Kitchin's extensions are useful, but big data also encompasses changing data practices and new forms of sociality. This vantage point is critical as it not only emphasizes the social life of these data, but also that big data encompasses the methods used to study them as well. In addition, placing primacy on classification via machine learning or other data science methods raises questions of epistemology and ontology that should not be glossed over (Murthy 2016).

Visual social media kicks up particular challenges in terms of big data. As Vis (2013) argues, visual social media are difficult types of content to text classified by machine learning, presenting challenges to deriving fine resolution in large data sets. In most cases, advanced, custom-tailored recognition algorithms or some form of hand coding would have to be used. Therefore, in commercial contexts, images with easily mineable metadata (tagged by users or by platform providers) are valued more (Vis 2013). Montgomery (2015) adds that "marketplace forces" are driving technology that can 'identify and target individuals through the photos they have posted of themselves, as well as images in pictures'. In cases where images cannot be automatically identified, the micro-work platform Amazon Mechanical Turk (AMT) has been used to achieve higher usable sample counts (Rashtchian et al. 2010). Others have opted for smaller random samples through hand coding of images by a research team (Morgan, Snelson/Elison-Bowers 2010).

More creative methods to study large image corpora have also been employed. For example, Hochman and Schwartz (2012), use aggregate big data methods to compare Instagram usage between Tokyo and New York City by creating montages of all posted images to discern an identifiable "local color". Clearly, big data methods vary from quantitative to more mixed or artistic methods, highlighting how difficult it is to frame not only what big data means, but also what the term means in the specific context of visual social media.

This is potentially compounded by an overabundance of visual social media material. Social researchers clearly want to interpret these data as visually-oriented social media activities may be transforming how people understand and experience events (both in crises and every day). In the case of occupy Wall Street, Milner (2013: 2357) argues that interpreting images (in his case, mimetic ones) is important to understanding "conversation between diverse positions". The proliferation of images in social media platforms is part of economic and social changes that are a product of the information age. Shifman (2012: 199) argues: "Whereas the old economic system focused on 'things', the most valuable resource in the information era is not information but the attention people pay to it." And images are an important part of garnering attention on social media platforms as Ringrose and Harvey's (2015) work on 'sexting images' reveals. Existing images need to be reposted or new images posted to keep or gain visibility. Feng et al. (2015) argue that "[b]ecause messages come to a user every day, new messages appearing above old messages, an information overload means any message, however popular, will rapidly lose its visibility." These changes in computer-mediated-communication have implications for social communication more broadly, including our interactions face-to-face (e.g. discussing the newest viral image or video with friends). Therefore, not only are large volumes of images important to everyday social media user practices, but big data methods need to be engaged with meaningfully in the digital humanities and social sciences. Otherwise, we risk not understanding changes in human communication, or letting purely computational methods dominate this field.

Instagram

There has been a proliferation of online socially-augmented applications that attempt to create social communities based on the sharing of various types of content with 'friends'/followers on those platforms or the public-at-large. Among the popular types of content shared in such communities are updates/messages (Twitter/Facebook), photo/visual media (Instagram/Snapchat/YouTube), and location (Foursquare). Instagram is a popular mobile photo sharing application that debuted in 2010. In April of 2012, Facebook bought the service for $1 billion. Instagram has over 500 million monthly active users with 80% of them outside of the US (Instagram 2016). It is compatible with a range of mobile platforms and devices. The application allows users to take pictures using their mobile device. They can apply filters to these photographs to customize their color, tone, and content amongst other things. These filter-applied images can then be shared on a variety of social media that have included Facebook, Twitter, Foursquare, and Weibo over the years. Users can also follow each other via Instagram.

The app's initial uniqueness, as Lister (2013: 11) argues, is its ability to "turn 'run-of-the-mill' snapshots into retro images". However, the platform quickly broadened from an app to allow people to apply image filters (particularly vintage 35mm film chemistries) and evolved into a mainstream photo sharing service. Instagram posts also tend to include an array of hashtags allowing for the image to become a 'network image' (Lister 2013: 4), highlighting the interconnectedness of posted image content. Images were easily networked across several social media platforms as well. As a result, a social network emerged to allow users to share pictures with each other. Instagram is one of the most popular visual media sharing applications and now generates a significant portion of Facebook's revenue (Verhage 2016). Historically, photos shared on Instagram are original photos taken by the user on their smartphone and are usually posted real time (Zappavigna 2016). Many Instagram images are also tagged with location information. In this sense, studying Instagram image streams can give one insights into what people are doing, and when and where – sometimes to the latitude and longitude – they are doing it.

Social Media and Disasters

A rich literature has emerged both around Instagram and Twitter use during disasters. Though work around Instagram and disasters is highly emergent, Twitter use during disasters has been studied in a variety of contexts. For example, Mendoza et al. (2010) studied tweets posted during the 2010 Chilean earthquake and argue that rumours are more likely to be identified and questioned on Twitter than truths during disasters. Following this thread of authenticity, Gupta et al. (2013) examine the spread of inaccurate/deceptive/misleading images on Twitter during Hurricane Sandy, focusing specifically on the height of storm activity (the night of October 29, 2012). They find that these images mostly spread through retweets and that 90 per cent of all retweets can be attributed to the top 30 users. Importantly, they find that users are often comfortable circulating images from sources they are not currently following. This is in distinction to the authority over images previously held by traditional broadcast and print media.

Mills et al. (2009) argue that Twitter has real utility "in time-pressured and information-critical situations." However, they note that, as the medium's user base increases, inaccurate information is more likely to appear and spread quickly. They find that Twitter is the leading informational site in the first hour of a situation and other media catch-up after that. Mills et al. argue that Twitter is particularly valuable for 'second or third waves of emergency response rather than disaster victims and first wave responders, depending on how dialed-in those people are to the network'. Indeed, part of the utility of any social medium during disasters is its usability as a disaster unfolds. Veinott et al. (2009) found that Twitter has utility as a 'lightweight, low bandwidth' broadcast tool, but there is a learning curve for best use practices during an emergency.

Similarly, Vieweg et al. (2010) compare two natural disasters – flooding of the Red River and a major grassfire in Oklahoma. They found that users had very different tweeting behaviours. Most people in the Red River area of North Dakota/Winnipeg had experienced a flood before. Additionally, the location of a river does not have the same unpredictability as a wildfire. They find that geolocated tweets and situational update tweets are more likely to be retweeted. Vieweg at al. categorize disaster-related communications into Preparation, Warning, Response to Warning, Hazard Locations, Advice, and Other Environmental Conditions. These studies not only point to discernible patterns in social media production and consumption during disasters, but emphasize that social media content can be coded into meaningful topical categories.

Methods

Data collection

We utilized Twitter's 'Streaming API' to collect tweets from 50 major US cities. We chose the most populous cities according to the 2011 Census Prediction, which estimates population increase based on the last full census (Wilson/United States Bureau of the Census 2012). Twitter allows for the collection of tweets from specified geographical 'bounding boxes', specified by a series of latitude and longitude coordinates. The Streaming API has three major functions: users, locations, or keywords. Following Vieweg et al.'s (2010) argument that geolocated tweets during a disaster are more likely to be retweeted, our study focuses on the Places object within the Twitter API, which allows for real-time delivery of tweets from these major cities to our database. Tweets were then filtered for three storm related terms: "hurricane", "storm" and "sandy". This search returned 142,768 tweets. With this geolocated sample, we isolated tweets that contained links to outside media. From there, we followed any links to Instagram photos embedded within the tweet. This search returned 11,964 Instagram images that we manually coded for study.

Coding methods

Due to the large volume of images we needed to interpret, our coding methods focused on motif categories rather than trying to interpret the nuances and idiosyncrasies of the images or their 'performative power' (Chouliaraki/Blaagaard 2013: 254). Following established methods of categorizing tweets into disaster-related bins (Vieweg et al. 2010), these images were then coded into separate disaster-related motif categories (see Figure 2 for a list of these categories). A team of six coded images following the same coding framework. Images that fit multiple codes were double coded, yielding a total of 15,924 coded instances.

The categories we used for coding were designed to relate to all three phases of Sandy: pre-storm, when Sandy made US landfall, and Sandy's aftermath. The categories in alphabetical order that we employed are detailed in Table 1. Figure 1 provides examples of posted images by coding category.

Code	Description
ad	images depicting commercial advertisements (not inclusive of relief-related campaigns which were categorized as 'relief')
animals	images depicting animals of any kind
damage	images depicting storm-related damage to the built environment or otherwise.
drink	images depicting beverages of any kind, alcoholic and non-alcoholic
food	images depicting perishable food, generally prepared food (not inclusive of canned goods or other non-perishable food; inclusive of restaurants)
gear	images depicting equipment and supplies (inclusive of water and non-perishable food used as emergency supplies)
macro	images depicting humorous macros, images that have a picture superimposed with text with a specific purpose of being funny.
other	images depicting anything not fitting into other specified coding categories
outside	images depicting the built environment, nature, or spaces/places not indoors
people	images depicting people (not inclusive of cartoon depictions of people; inclusive of selfies, individuals, and groups of people)
relief	images depicting relief efforts and relief campaigns (inclusive of screenshots of relief campaigns)

Table 1: Image coding categories.

Results

Frequency Results

Our data clearly illustrates that storm-related Instagram images are concentrated over a three-day period (see Figure 2). On the day of the storm, an increase in activity on Twitter occurred as users weighed in on the storm, including those far outside its path. This fits with previous work on Twitter and disasters which indicates Twitter frequency is generally highest the day a disaster hits (Hughes/Palen 2009). Unsurprisingly, the modal frequency of tweets was immediately after the US landfall of Hurricane Sandy (see Figure 2). Users at the peak of the storm, which occurred when Sandy made US landfall, were likely to post photos at a higher rate. On October 28, 2012, Instagram users posted photos regarding supplies for when the hurricane hit, 'Sandy parties' in restaurants and homes, and of friends and family. Sandy parties were common subjects of Instagram images. They featured groups of people eating and drinking before they had to face the predicted impact of Sandy. In terms of supplies to prepare for the storm (what we categorized as 'gear'), it was clear that users felt anxious about how long the storm would be impacting the Eastern Seaboard. Many images were posted of storm rations, food, and forms of entertainment to keep people busy as they stayed indoors.

Figure 1: Examples of Instagram images by category.

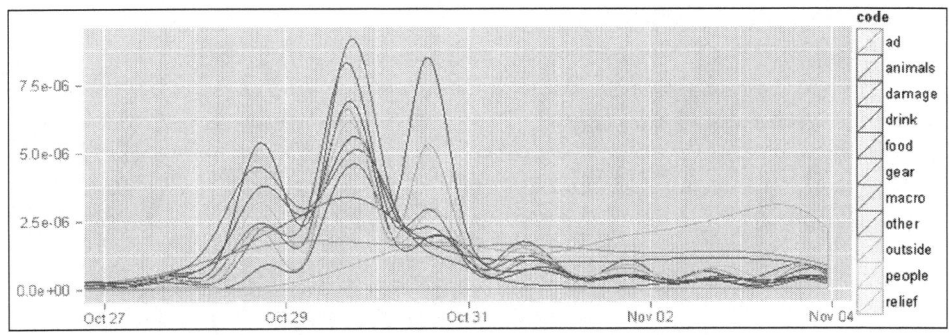

Figure 2: Frequency of selected coded categories by date.

On October 29, 2012, the day Sandy made US landfall, humorous images (what we term 'macro' as the majority of images in this category were image macros), were widely circulated. As Figure 2 indicates, the modal category on October 29 was macro. Some humorous images started 'trending', becoming the most circulated images. This is an important finding as macro images have been previously found to be important to defining events and movements on social media. For example, Milner (2013: 2358) cites the example of a macro-like poster image of a ballerina dancing on top of Wall Street's Charging Bull statue, which became emblematic for the Occupy Wall Street movement.

Instagram images perhaps also enabled users to collectively cope by making light the severity of what was to come, similar to the use of humour in other disasters including 9/11 (Kuipers 2005) and the Challenger explosion (Smyth 1986). Other work on images circulating on social media during Sandy indicate the prevalence of humorous images (e. g. with Godzilla and Jaws in front of the Statue of Liberty), but also highlight the circulation of dramatic, non-fiction images (Burgess/Vis/Bruns 2012).

On October 30, 2012, the aftermath of Sandy, users began to focus on the built environment, with specific attention paid to the categories of 'damage' and 'outside', findings, consistent with other work on images during Sandy (Burgess/Vis/Bruns 2012). We found a discernible trend of circulating iconic images, where particular images became signatures of the storm on Instagram. This parallels work on visual cultures where, during 9/11, the 'visual impact' of the image of planes crashing into the twin towers was tremendous, both in the short and long-term (Young 2007). In the case of Sandy, it was of the crane from outside the new World Trade Center tower and the façade of a Chelsea apartment that had been ripped off. These became iconic images of the storm seen from the vantage point of Instagram images posted on Twitter.

In images depicting external damage (what we term 'outside'), the focus was of trees coming down, flooding, and damage to the built environment. What is interesting to note is that these images are prevalent in the immediate aftermath of this disaster, providing a glimpse into the vantage point of those living within disaster-affected areas. In terms of images related to 'relief' efforts, we saw a jump in frequency on October 30 that did not fully peak until November 3. Some users took pictures of themselves at the Sandy telethon. Others took screenshots of their Red Cross donations and posted them on Instagram. The latter was particularly popular and resembles peer-motivated behavior seen in other events such as the Obama badges used by users on their social media profiles during the 2008 American presidential election (Harfoush 2009: 27).

The longevity of categories such as damage, outside, and people (as seen in Figure 2) illustrates that the categories had different meanings both in terms of when they were posted (specifically the stage of Sandy) as well as the fact that these categories remained important throughout the disaster. Users posting Instagram images on Twitter therefore had an interest and commitment to documenting their own disaster experiences (whether these were lighthearted prior to Sandy's landfall, about getting back to daily routines (such as getting pets out of the house), or commenting on damage in Sandy's aftermath). In other words, these users kept these types of image categories persistent through Sandy, representing an important collective effort.

	Frequency	Percent
ad	247	1.6%
animals	397	2.5%
damage	2035	12.8%
drink	1217	7.6%
food	1026	6.4%
gear	208	1.3%
macro	381	2.4%
other	1155	7.3%
outside	5623	35.3%
people	3366	21.1%
relief	269	1.7%
Total	**15924**	**100.0%**

Table 2: Frequencies of coded images.

Table 2 illustrates the frequency of codes applied to images. These frequencies are important as aggregated frequencies in some ways help tell alternative stories of Sandy than mainstream accounts. Specifically, there is a very high frequency of people, food, and drink for example and low frequencies for relief and gear. Additionally, what is noteworthy is that categories such as relief and gear do have frequencies that are lower than we might expect. However, damage does have a relatively high frequency and this indicates that individuals are keen to document their disaster experience, something also supported by the higher levels of frequencies of outside and people. The macro coded category has a relatively high frequency, when one considers this category is based on macro images, images with superimposed text, rather than humorous images as a whole. Indeed, macro images have a higher frequency than both relief and gear. The same, unexpectedly, is true for animals. These image frequencies help sketch an outline of the types of narratives unfolding during Sandy and the types of things people are focusing on representing in their images, potentially suggesting unique views of the disaster, that do include the destruction wreaked by Sandy, but also the human, everyday side such as selfies with friends, pet images, and sharing funny macros.

Category Correlations

As part of our analysis, we correlated categories in our data to investigate whether particular categories were co-occurring. This analysis not only produced some useful insights into exploring Instagram use during Hurricane Sandy, but also provided evidence of how images often perform multiple tasks. As Table 3 and Figure 3 indicate, we found images correlated across coded categories.

People	Outside	r = 0.86**
Food	Drink	r = 0.85**
Outside	Damage	r = 0.84**
People	Food	r = 0.81**
People	Drink	r = 0.78**
Animals	Outside	r = 0.73**
Food	Outside	r = 0.73**
Relief	Macro	r = 0.0
Food	Relief	r = −0.06
Relief	Drink	r = −0.09

(*p < .05, ** p < .001)

Table 3. Select coded category correlations.

Table 3 highlights selected correlations and Figure 3 illustrates all correlations. Our results indicate discernible patterns of co-occurrence within Instagram images we coded. Of particular note is that more than a quarter of coded images tend to have co-occurrence rather than involving single categories. Indeed, the vast majority of categories show significant co-occurrence (at p < .05 and p < .001). This is important as many images do not tend to be singular in their focus, but are representations of multiple aspects of the disaster experience.

Figure 3: Correlations of all coded categories.

There are also several important instances of an absence of correlation. In particular, the lack of correlation between relief and macro is noteworthy as it signals a sort of taboo or no-go area regarding the Sandy relief efforts (especially the telethon). What emerges is an underlying understanding that relief efforts were a serious endeavour and key to larger, long-term post-Sandy recovery. The lack of correlation of relief with food and drink was expected as Sandy parties generally took place before US landfall. Every other category except for 'ad' has a significant level of correlation with macro, indicating that humour is widespread across Sandy-related motif categories, but not in the case of relief-oriented images. This is an important finding.

Temporality

Ultimately, we found that the temporality of tweets was a fundamental, constant variable across our research questions for understanding the context of tweets and serves as a key means to understand how Twitter users responded to Hurricane Sandy at each phase. We found that the highest levels of Twitter activity occurred when Sandy made US landfall. After October 29, there is a significant drop off in storm-related tweets, suggesting that Twitter users prioritize the here and now. Twitter's prompt of 'What's happening' encourages a focus on one's immediate environment and to tweet about one's experience in the present. Our collected data suggests that particular types of subjects are captured in posted images and, collectively, certain narratives emerge at particular points of time (e.g. the importance of meeting with friends prior to Sandy's US landfall and the need to get on with daily routines such as walking one's dog after Sandy made landfall). In other words, the highly temporal nature of social media platforms means that there are many narratives unfolding, but that there are also group-level narratives and perspectives that can be identified. As is the case with other events on Twitter (Murthy 2013), most users were quick to move on to a new story once the storm had passed. This was partially a function of the 2012 presidential election on the horizon, but is more attributable to the fact that Twitter is event/trend driven (Naaman, Becker/Gravano 2011).

However, once Sandy made US landfall, the focus of tweets moved from humorous macros to serious reflections of the real damage caused by Sandy. Many tweets during this time included information from weather sites that tracked the path of the storm as it made its way up the US eastern seaboard. As we used geolocated tweets, we were also able to see that Twitter users outside of the Tri-State area (New York, New Jersey, and Connecticut) generally tweeted prior and during US landfall, but their tweeting is never, relatively speaking, frequent. We compared several unaffected US cities to New York and saw that their tweeting pattern was largely unchanged during Sandy (Murthy/Gross 2016). However, to some extent, this confirms a certain necessary co-presence of tweets during disasters or, put another way, out of sight, out of mind. In addition, we wanted to contextualize the images we collected both in terms of time and space. Specifically, we are claiming that these images help tell a story of how Sandy was experience by its victims in the Tri-State area. The fact that the modal frequency in our data is when Sandy hit the Tri-State area and our data confirms the majority of location-enabled tweets as originating from there as well. Ultimately, our empirical data indicates that users posting Instagram images on Twitter followed a collective temporal pattern, marking particular stages of Sandy: pre-US landfall, US landfall, and aftermath. These stages also correspond to traditional temporal demarcations of hurricanes (Brommer/Senkbeil 2010).

Discussion

For the US, Hurricane Sandy was one of the most devastating storms since Hurricane Katrina. In the days leading to Sandy's US landfall, professional and citizen meteorologists were actively tweeting within Sandy-related hashtags offering forecasts of when Sandy would make landfall and what types of inclement weather the storm would bring. All major news outlets were covering the storm well before US landfall and there was a general climate of anxiety in this coverage. Residents of the Tri-State area responded by stockpiling storm supplies such as clean water, dried food, and changes of clothes. Tweets from official weather services such as the National Oceanic and Atmospheric Administration's Twitter account mixed with unofficial weather reports on Twitter. Often, official and unofficial reports were blurred, inaccurate, or confusing and this caused palpable anxiety amongst Twitter users. It is also unsurprising that humour, a genre generally popular on Twitter and Instagram was deployed as part of a mode to engage with this anxiety.

The role of self and time

Previous studies of Instagram highlight that selfies, images of friends, and images of activities being undertaken are the top three types of images found in Instagram data (Hu, Manikonda, and Kambhampati 2014). These three categories tend to place primacy on representing what an Instagram user is experiencing from their vantage point. The role of 'selfies', the taking of photographs, which include oneself (Tiidenberg 2015), is important to the placement of self within these contexts in Sandy-related images. Images of the outside, including damage to the built environment tended to include people, as our correlations found. This indicates that the experience of placing users within the physical context of the disaster was considered important. Of note, in our findings is that the marked high frequency of humorous tweets occurs before Sandy's US landfall during this heightened state of anxiety, indicating that significant numbers of sampled users were responding to Sandy's forecasted damage through humour. Interestingly, this was simultaneously semi-private and public. The former mostly involved selfies, mentions of friends, and images of friends, family, and local places. The latter primarily involved image macros.

An important finding of this study is that embedded Instagram images in tweets during Sandy often had a co-occurrence of coded categories. For example, images including pets outside were also frequent during Sandy's aftermath as users began to navigate affected areas with their pets. The posting of pet-related also came from people confined at home with their pets providing a diversion as the disaster unfolded. This is an important conclusion in that the images be posted tend to engage with multiple aspects of the lived disaster experience. Another finding is that Instagram images posted during Sandy exhibit identifiable trends before, during, and after Sandy made US landfall. This illustrates that social media including Instagram images posted on Twitter are sensitive to the distinct phases of disasters. Users are likely synchronously posting their content to social media from their mobile devices. This provides new ways of meaningfully narrating one's disaster experience visually in real-time.

The role of humour and inaccurate/deceptive/misleading images

Though many first-hand experiences are clearly being portrayed, Instagram images posted on Twitter also included significant numbers of inaccurate/deceptive/misleading images, especially on the day Sandy made US landfall (Gupta et al. 2013, Madrigal 2012). Though beyond the remit of this study, we also anecdotally saw a reasonable frequency of these types of images in our data. However, we did not code for this category, but believe that future work in this area would be beneficial for not only understanding when these types of images were circulating (i.e. stage of the disaster), but also their uses and impacts.

The importance of humour within our collected data was an interesting finding. As our case study was based on the convergence between Instagram and Twitter, we were able to see humour play into this cross-platform space and become networked into Twitter via hashtags. For example, some image macros featured celebrities (e.g. Sean Bean – Eddard Stark from Game of Thrones) and had hashtags on Twitter such as #GameOfThrones; #ImminentNed (the name given to this macro); and #BraceYourself. SpongeBob SquarePants image macros eventually joined this pre-landfall stream via the fictional character Sandy Cheeks and SpongeBob-related hashtags such as #sandycheeks parodying Sandy were appended. Other images played to the humorous hashtag '#frankenstorm' as the storm took place around Halloween in the US and image macros included clips from the 1931 original *Frankenstein* film. Many images also parodied the character Sandy from the classic hit movie/musical *Grease* and also incorporated humorous hashtags. Even on the day of US landfall, we expected to find more images chronicling the destruction and impact on the built environment or of trees falling down, humorous images were more frequent, highlighting a different, lighthearted, representation of their disaster experiences. (That being said, images of damage caused by the disaster were the most frequent images across the entire data set).

Implications for visual social media research

The landscape for conducting visual social media research is always a moving target. This is partially why research has often avoided interpreting visual content. In addition, image-oriented social media platforms such as Instagram and Snapchat have restricted or inaccessible APIs. This case study was conducted at a unique point in time when Instagram content was being integrated with Twitter feeds and researchers could easily collect these data by accessing the Twitter API. After its acquisition by Facebook in April 2012, Instagram began a slow divorce with Twitter shutting off friend finding functions in July 2012 and ultimately completely shutting off image sharing into Twitter feeds in December, 2012. Therefore, just a month after Sandy, Instagram and Twitter fully parted ways. Perceived commercial competition in the social media market and its acquisition by Facebook likely influenced Instagram's decision to close its API except for paid access in June, 2016.

Through this empirical case study, we have argued that part of considering the politics of big data in regards to visual social media involves us taking stock of the real external challenges to these types of research, both in terms of stricter API access as well as having to innovate research methods to overcome these difficulties. But, a payoff of this is that alternative narratives that emerge may help tell different stories to those portrayed by professional journalists, relief organizations, or institutional bodies. It is important for these voices and stories to be represented alongside mainstream accounts in order to provide a more holistic narrative of the disaster experience, that includes humour, pets, and even drunken parties before Sandy made landfall. However, social researchers may be placed in the situation of having to purchase visual social media data to accomplish these ends and this has real implications for what types of researchers can actually undertake these studies.

Conclusions

This article uses a case study of geolocated Instagram images shared on Twitter immediately before, during, and after Hurricane Sandy to explore the behavioural dynamic of disaster-related image sharing behavior during the storm. We studied the content of 11,964 images and explored how and what types of images users shared during the storm. Hurricane Sandy-related images were posted at a rate of 10 per second on Instagram (Laird 2012). Our case study is unique in that Sandy is perhaps the first major US disaster where Instagram played a major role in victims' social experience, and Instagram images were integrated with Twitter. This case study enabled a large set of images to be collected that were networked images, crossing both Twitter and Instagram. They became part of larger Twitter and Instagram discourses and these converged data were collected prior to Instagram tightening and eventually closing down its application programming interface (API). Most social media platforms are walled gardens for commercial reasons and this case study reveals how users are behaving in a somewhat convergent social media space. In addition, posted image volume may have been higher as a product of this confluence.

Images perform multiple tasks during a disaster. By coding images, we were able to better understand some of the multiple functions they performed. These images emphasize the human side of Sandy and how people experienced the disaster first hand. The high frequency of images with both food and drink as well as using animals in humorous images illustrates individuals, in some ways, carried on with our daily lives even in the face of large-scale destruction. However, empirical studies of what types of images are being produced and consumed remain limited. This is attributable to both the challenges of obtaining visual social media data (such as Instagram's closing of its API) to the difficulty of interpreting social media (e.g. the lack of easy content classification). Because the use of images during disasters has implications ranging from emergency services provisioning to understanding people's varied disaster experiences to understanding user content and practices, it is important to develop ways of tackling these obstacles.

Unlike other work on disasters, our study finds that in the case of Hurricane Sandy, many Instagram images posted on Twitter reflect the vantage point of disaster victims rather than official responders as Mills et al. (2009) found in previous disasters. This is likely due to users posting images right as Sandy made US landfall. In this sense, we found that time is a crucial variable. Specifically, pre-social media reporting usually defined the narrative of disasters, but it was often difficult for journalists to get to the scene first. With contemporary social media platforms, everyone is potentially a citizen journalist and time becomes critical to what images end up representing the disaster. Images can circulate virally on social media before even a single reporter arrives at the scene. This is not only true in highly visible types of damage like the façade of a Chelsea apartment that had been ripped off, but also is true in more banal disaster experiences such as electricity shortages. In the case of the latter, images of New Yorkers stringing together extension cords to charge their phones and laptops helps us see Sandy through the eyes of those experiencing the disaster first hand. This potential shift of representation to social media users away from journalists is significant.

It is also clear that these images provide a sort of counter-narrative to mainstream media accounts. By studying these large sets of images, we are able to potentially help tell a different part of the Sandy narrative that may also provide more humanizing and holistic accounts. For example, these images tell a story of how those in the New York area were anxious prior to Sandy's landfall and threw Sandy parties, met with friends to have dinner or grab drinks. Then when Sandy made US landfall, there was major damage, but disaster victims also took their pets outside, took selfies in front of smashed cars, and struggled with power, water, and food shortages. Social researchers should pursue work to give voice to these alternative depictions of disasters and other crises.

Our findings also highlight that Twitter's use – in all phases of Sandy – is generally not geared towards interacting with major relief organizations such as the Red Cross. Rather, the medium affords different uses. For example, the ease by which users can share images and check into locations via Foursquare made it seamless for users to not only continue these routine habits, but actually perhaps increase these behaviours – especially photo sharing. Disaster sociology literature emphasizes how our use of the word 'disaster' refers to 'a distinct event that disrupts the accustomed flow of everyday life' (Erikson cited in Bruhn 2011, 112). However, our findings suggest that social media-based routines are not particularly interrupted, though they do have different subjects for photos and locations for check-ins. These findings help highlight the importance of critical empirical-based big data work to better understanding what latent narratives may exist within visual social media data. Our work also reveals the potential richness of what can be derived from visual social media data, while simultaneously highlighting the implications of these types of work. Historically, disasters were understood through top-down perspectives, but large volumes of social media data can change the politics of representing disasters. Specifically, visual social media data during disasters can reflect a 'vernacular' (Murray 2013) understanding of the disaster, which rather than glossing over humour, pets, and other everyday experiences, draws our attention to them.

Acknowledgements

The authors are grateful for the generous feedback received by reviewers. We also benefited from questions and comments on a work in progress version of this article presented at the 6th International *Social Media & Society* conference held in Toronto, Canada, July 27–29, 2015.

References

boyd, danah/Crawford, Kate (2012): "Critical Questions for Big Data." In: Information, Communication & Society 15/5, pp. 662–679.
Brommer, David M./Senkbeil, Jason C. (2010): "Pre-landfall evacuee perception of the meteorological hazards associated with Hurricane Gustav." In: Natural hazards 55/2, pp. 353–369.
Bruhn, John G. (2011): The Sociology of Community Connections, Berlin-Heidelberg: Springer. Burgess, Jean/Vis, Farida/Bruns, Axel (2012): "Hurricane Sandy: the most tweeted pictures." In: The Guardian, November 6 (https://www.theguardian.com/news/datablog/gallery/2012/nov/06/hurricane-sandy-tweeted-pictures)
Chouliaraki, Lillie/Blaagaard, Bolette (2013): "Special Issue: The ethics of images." In: Visual Communication 12/3, pp. 253–259.
Cook, James (2016): "Instagram made a change that stopped lots of third-party apps from working." In: Business Insider, 4 June (http://www.businessinsider.de/instagram-made-a-change-that-stopped-lots-of-third-party-apps-from-working-2016-6)
Feng, Ling et al. (2015): "Competing for attention in social media under information overload conditions." In: PloS one 10/7.

Gupta, Aditi/Lamba, Hemank/Kumaraguru, Ponnurangam/Joshi, Anupam (2013): "Faking Sandy: characterizing and identifying fake images on twitter during hurricane Sandy." In: Proceedings of the 22nd international conference on World Wide Web, pp. 729–736.

Harfoush, Rahaf (2009): Yes We Did! An inside look at how social media built the Obama brand, San Francisco: New Riders.

Hochman, Nadav/Schwartz, Raz (2012): "Visualizing instagram: Tracing cultural visual rhythms." In: Proceedings of the Workshop on Social Media Visualization (SocMedVis) in conjunction with the Sixth International AAAI Conference on Weblogs and Social Media (ICWSM–12).

Hogan, Bernie/Quan-Haase, Anabel (2010): "Persistence and change in social media." In: Bulletin of Science, Technology & Society 30/5, pp. 309–315.

Hu, Yuheng/Manikonda, Lydia/Kambhampati, Subbarao (2014): "What We Instagram: A First Analysis of Instagram Photo Content and User Types." In: Proceedings of the Eighth International AAAI Conference on Weblogs and Social Media.

Hughes, Amanda Lee/Palen, Leysia (2009): "Twitter adoption and use in mass convergence and emergency events." In: International Journal of Emergency Management 6/3, pp. 248–260.

Instagram (2016): "Press News." September 02 (https://www.instagram.com/press/).

Kaisler, Stephen/Armour, Frank/Espinosa, Juan Antonio/Money, William (2013): "Big data: Issues and challenges moving forward." In: 46th Hawaii International Conference on System Sciences (HICSS).

Kitchin, Rob (2014): "Big Data, new epistemologies and paradigm shifts." In: Big Data & Society 1/1.

Kuipers, Giselinde (2005): "'Where Was King Kong When We Needed Him?' Public Discourse, Digital Disaster Jokes, and the Functions of Laughter after 9/11." In: The Journal of American Culture 28/1, pp. 70–84.

Laird, S. (2012): "Instagram Users Share 10 Hurricane Sandy Photos Per Second." In: Mashable (http://mashable.com/2012/10/29/instagram-hurricane-sandy/#AOTCvPj4Zkqu).

Lister, Martin (2013): The photographic image in digital culture, London: Routledge.

Lupton, Deborah (2015): Digital sociology, London: Routledge.

Madrigal, Alexis C. (2012): "Sorting the Real Sandy Photos From the Fakes." In: The Atlantic, Oct. 29.

Manovich, Lev (2012): "Trending: the promises and challenges of big social data." In: Matthew K. Gold (ed.): Debates in the digital humanities, Minneapolis: University of Minnesota Press, pp. 460–475.

Mendoza, Marcelo/Poblete, Barbara/Castillo, Carlos (2010): "Twitter Under Crisis: Can we trust what we RT?" In: Proceedings of the first workshop on social media analytics.

Mills, Alexander/Rui, Chen/Lee, Jin-Kyu/Rao, H. Raghav (2009): "Web 2.0 emergency applications: How useful can Twitter be for emergency response?" In: Journal of Information Privacy and Security 5/3, pp. 3–26.

Milner, Ryan M. (2013): "Pop polyvocality: Internet memes, public participation, and the Occupy Wall Street movement." In: International Journal of Communication 7/34.

Montgomery, Kathryn C. (2015): "Youth and surveillance in the Facebook era: Policy interventions and social implications." In: Telecommunications Policy 39/9, pp. 771–786.

Morgan, Elizabeth M/Snelson, Chareen/Elison-Bowers, Patt (2010): "Image and video disclosure of substance use on social media websites." In: Computers in Human Behavior 26/6, pp. 1405–1411.

Murray, Susan (2013): "New media and vernacular photography: Revisiting Flickr." In: Martin Lister (ed.): The photographic image in digital culture, London: Routledge, pp. 165–182.

Murthy, Dhiraj (2013): Twitter: Social communication in the Twitter age, Chichester: John Wiley & Sons.

Murthy, Dhiraj (2016): "The ontology of tweets: Mixed methods approaches to the study of Twitter" In: Luke Sloan/Anabel Quan-Hasse (eds.): The SAGE Handbook of Social Media Research, London: Sage.

Murthy, Dhiraj/Bowman, Sawyer A. (2014): "Big Data solutions on a small scale: Evaluating accessible high-performance computing for social research." In: Big Data & Society 1/2.

Murthy, Dhiraj/Gross, Alexander J. (2016): "Social media processes in disasters: Implications of emergent technology use." In: Social Science Research, in press, doi: http://dx.doi.org/10.1016/j.ssresearch.2016.09.015.

Naaman, Mor/Becker, Hila/Gravano, Luis (2011): "Hip and trendy: Characterizing emerging trends on Twitter." In: Journal of the American Society for Information Science and Technology 62/5, pp. 902–918.

Rashtchian, Cyrus/Young, Peter/Hodosh, Micah/Hockenmaier, Julia (2010): "Collecting image annotations using Amazon's Mechanical Turk." In: Proceedings of the NAACL HLT 2010 Workshop on Creating Speech and Language Data with Amazon's Mechanical Turk, Los Angeles, California.

Ringrose, Jessica/Harvey, Laura (2015): "Boobs, back-off, six packs and bits: Mediated body parts, gendered reward, and sexual shame in teens' sexting images." In: Continuum 29/2, pp. 205–217.

Ruppert, Evelyn (2015): "Big data economies and ecologies." In: Linda McKie/Louise Ryan (eds.): An End to the Crisis of Empirical Sociology? Trends and Challenges in Social Research, Abingdon-Oxford: Routledge, pp. 13–28.

Seltzer, Emily K./Jean, N. S./Kramer-Golinkoff, Emily/Asch, David A./Merchant, R. M. (2015): "The content of social media's shared images about Ebola: a retrospective study." In: Public Health 129/9, pp. 1273–1277.

Shifman, Limor (2012): "An anatomy of a YouTube meme." In: New media & Society 14/2, pp. 187–203.
Shifman, Limor (2014): "The cultural logic of photo-based meme genres." In: Journal of Visual Culture 13/3, pp. 340–358.
Smyth, Willie (1986): "Challenger Jokes and the Humor of Disaster." In: Western Folklore 45/4, pp. 243–260.
Tiidenberg, Katrin (2015): "Boundaries and conflict in a NSFW community on tumblr: The meanings and uses of selfies." In: New Media & Society, pp. 1–16.
Veinott, Beth/Cox, Donald/Mueller, Shane (2009): "Social media supporting disaster response: Evaluation of a lightweight collaborative tool." In: Proceedings of NDM9, the 9th International Conference on Naturalistic Decision Making.
Verhage, Julie (2016): "Credit Suisse says Instagram is going to have a huge year." In: *Bloomberg Markets*, April 19 (http://www.bloomberg.com/news/articles/2016-04-19/credit-suisse-says-instagram-will-generate-over-three-times-as-much-revenue-as-facebook-paid-to-acquire-it).
Vieweg, Sarah/Hughes, Amanda L./Starbird, Kate/Palen, Leysia (2010): "Microblogging during two natural hazards events: What twitter may contribute to situational awareness." In: Proceedings of the SIGCHI conference on human factors in computing systems.
Vis, Farida (2013): "A critical reflection on Big Data: Considering APIs, researchers and tools as data makers." In: First Monday 18/10.
Wilson, Steven G./United States Bureau of the Census (2012): Patterns of Metropolitan and Micropolitan Population Change: 2000 to 2010.
Xinpeng, L. Liao/Pradip, Chitrakar/Chengcui, Zhang/Gary, Warner (2015): "Object-of-Interest Retrieval in Social Media Image Databases for e-Crime Forum Detection." In: International Journal of Multimedia Data Engineering and Management (IJMDEM) 6/3, pp. 32–50.
Yates, Dave/Paquette, Scott (2011): "Emergency knowledge management and social media technologies: A case study of the 2010 Haitian earthquake." In: International journal of information management 31/1, pp. 6–13.
Young, Alison (2007): "Images in the aftermath of trauma: Responding to September 11th." In: Crime, Media, Culture 3/1, pp. 30–48.
Zappavigna, Michele (2016): "Social media photography: construing subjectivity in Instagram images." In: Visual Communication 15/3, pp. 271–292.
Zhenguo, Yang et al. (2015): "Semi-Supervised Multimodal Fusion Model for Social Event Detection on Web Image Collections." In: International Journal of Multimedia Data Engineering and Management (IJMDEM) 6/4, pp. 1–22.

Entering the Field

Group Privacy in Times of Big Data
A Literature Review

Paula Helm[1]

Abstract

New technologies pose new challenges on the protection of privacy and they stimulate new debates on the scope of privacy. Such debates usually concern the individuals' right to control the flow of his or her personal information. The article however discusses new challenges posed by new technologies in terms of their impact on groups and their privacy. Two main challenges are being identified in this regard, both having to do with the formation of groups through the involvement of algorithms and the lack of civil awareness regarding the consequences of this involvement. On the one hand, there is the phenomenon of groups being created on the basis of big data without the members of such groups being aware of having been assigned and being treated as part of a certain group. Here, the challenge concerns the limits of personal law, manifesting with the disability of individuals to address possible violations of their right to privacy since they are not aware of them. On the other hand, commercially driven Websites influence the way in which groups form, grow and communicate when doing this online and they do this in such subtle way, that members oftentimes do not take into account this influence. This is why one could speak of a kind of domination here, which calls for legal regulation. The article presents different approaches addressing and dealing with those two challenges, discussing their strengths and weaknesses. Finally, a conclusion gathers the insights reached by the different approaches discussed and reflects on future challenges for further research on group privacy in times of big data.

Keywords: Group Privacy, Algorithms, Group Theory, Group Rights, Digital Age

---

1   Paula Helm has submitted her paper on her own initiative.

Introduction

Technical developments are notorious for stimulating new debates on the boundaries and values of privacy. For instance, the famous claim for a "right to be let alone", formulated by two lawyers in 1890, was triggered by a case of wire-tapping (Warren/Brandeis 1890). With the right to be let alone, Warren/Brandeis aimed at strengthening defence-rights of the individual vis-à-vis the state. More recently, ground-breaking developments in information and communication technology, especially with the application of algorithms that collect and sort massive amounts of data, have given rise to a new wave of privacy concerns. The liberal idea of the individual's right to defence against the state still lies at the heart of these concerns.

However, this idea has been subject to much criticism for being too narrow (Shoeman 1985, Fuchs 2011, Bennet 2011, Cohen 2012, Helm 2016, Seubert/Becker 2016, Sevignani 2016). The critics have been provoked by phenomena such as mass-surveillance, brought about through new technologies and obviously pointing to the social and democratic relevance of data-mining. This clearly brings to light the need for an understanding of privacy-protection as a matter not only of individual choice-making but also social and political responsibility. Big and open data practices hence provoke a shift of focus, thereby also taking collective and social dimensions of privacy into account (Petronio 2002, Regan 2002, boyd 2014, Wolf/Willaert/Pierson 2014, Roberts 2014, Mokrosinska/Rössler 2015, Stahl 2016). Towards a collective conception, some privacy-scholars claim for instance to reach beyond the liberal idea of personal defence vis-à-vis the state by additionally taking into account the ever-increasing need for collective defence against powerful corporations as well (Gusy/Eichenhover/Schulte 2016). In terms of privacy, this concerns corporations who collect and sell massive amounts of data (Rössler 2015: 141–161).

The underlying conviction behind the idea that societies need to be able to defend themselves against the data-processing practices of not only state agencies but also private corporations and the potential cooperation between such power-players is an understanding of privacy as a fundamental resource of democratic societies.[2] Recent shifts in privacy scholarship can be considered as expressions of this conviction. Accordingly, it is necessary to call for a new examination of the group privacy-concept, which in its traditional sense needs to be considered as a mere add-on to individual privacy, thus failing to reflect the collective dimensions at stake. In this article I will review different research on group privacy that has been provoked by big data.

---

[2] In this regard, see for instance the work that is being undertaken by the research project "Transformations of Privacy". ULR: http://www.strukturwandeldesprivaten.de/index_eng.htm

To do so, I will start by briefly sketching out what I suggest calling the traditional notion of group privacy, referring back to a book written by Edward Bloustein in 1978. I will confront this traditional notion with a number of recent publications all pointing at the need for further research on the matter of group privacy in a digital age (2). In the main part of this article, I will proceed by discussing three different approaches to group privacy in the digital age in more detail (3): Linnet Taylor on the ethics of tracking mobility, Allessandro Mantelero on the collective dimension of data protection and Albert Ingold on group rights in the digital age.

All three approaches provide potentially fruitful contributions to a discussion that aims at developing an understanding of group privacy which takes into account groups qua groups, thus overcoming an individual-centric notion of group privacy. I chose to discuss especially those three in more detail, because I found that while all put forward important arguments, they are at the same time lacking crucial aspects in their studies which are – then again – covered by the other approaches discussed here. By reviewing them together, this article aims to show how the three chosen approaches can complement each other in a very fruitful way.

Linnet Taylor's empirical study on mobile tracking in Africa will be discussed first since her insights make very clear the urgency of framing group privacy as a matter of societal and political relevance. Allessandro Montelero, whose research will be discussed next, provides an overview of the field by suggesting possible starting points for a systematic approach to a new concept of group privacy rights. Finally, an article written by Albert Ingold will be reviewed. It presents a very creative and innovative approach to group rights in the digital age, by taking up central problems, which can be considered as blind spots within the other two approaches. However, as we will see, Ingolds' considerations need to be revisited very critically with regard to possible practical consequences that might follow from his theoretical proposals. In the discussion section (4) I will reflect on the question of how far all three approaches present important contributions to the question of group privacy in a digital age. Finally, I will discuss how they could be interlinked in order to develop a concept of group privacy that could do justice to what is at stake in current times, times of big data (5).

Background

The idea of Group Privacy originally goes back to Edward Bloustein, who was the first to argue that an individual right to privacy should become applicable to group contexts. In his book "Individual and Group Privacy" (1978), Bloustein firstly outlines what he understands under the concept of "individual privacy". This he does by referring to Warren & Brandeis's "right to be let alone". Secondly he introduces a right to group privacy, which he describes as the "right to huddle"

(p. 123). I argue that Bloustein's concept needs to be considered as dated, in that it does not suffice to meet the threats posed for groups in the digital age. This is mainly because Bloustein's approach is limited in two regards.

The first concerns Bloustein's attitude towards group rights. In explicitly referring to himself as an individualist who rejects holism, he consequently dismisses the idea of groups having a right qua group and indeed does not even give this option further thought. Instead, when speaking about a right to group privacy, Bloustein is exclusively concerned with the individual's right to privacy. He defines group privacy as a *"form of privacy that people seek in their associations with others. Group Privacy is an attribute of individuals in association with another within a group, rather than an attribute of the group itself."* (p. 124). Bloustein's innovative notion towards group privacy focuses exclusively on the individual deserving privacy protection not only when acting alone but also when acting from within group contexts. However, it does not concern the group itself and in light of this, Bloustein's approach to group privacy is to be considered rather as an add-on to the concept of individual privacy than a discrete concept in its own right. The second reason why Bloustein's traditional notion of group privacy seems to be too narrow can be found in its underlying understanding of privacy. As it concerns only individual defence rights, it needs to be considered as individualistic, blinding out important collective dimensions of privacy.

Since Bloustein's concept of group privacy is based on an individualistic understanding of privacy and since it is narrowed in reducing group rights to individual rights, it fails to face important problems involved with group privacy in the digital age. This is why a new debate on group privacy is urgently needed. In this I follow Luciano Floridi, who has called for an updated understanding of group privacy that overcomes an "atomistic ontology" (Floridi 2015: p. 2). As one step in this direction, Floridi – together with Linnet Taylor and Bart van der Sloot – is working on an anthology of group privacy. His aim is to collect different kinds of research that together reflect the variety of challenges facing group privacy, brought about by new data technologies (Taylor/Floridi/van der Sloot est. 2017). While this volume is still awaited, Floridi already recognises the need for further research on the matter by discussing it in a recent literature review on "the ethics of big data", co-authored with Brent D. Mittelstadt (2015). The idea and concept of the review is not only to provide a narrative of existing literature but also to point at other areas not yet acknowledged but requiring attention. In terms of group privacy, the authors make clear that further research is needed. They identify foreseeable ethical problems arising from big data practices connected to the group-level. In this regard they see in "group privacy rights" a potential measure "that could restrict the flow and acceptable uses of aggregated datasets and profiling" (Mittelstadt/Floridi 2015: p. 327). However, they do not follow this line of thought any further, but instead merely point to its potential.

Mittelstadt/Floridi's drawing on the ethical potential of group privacy rights is concerned with the data-processing practices of powerful entities. It aims at regulating power-imbalances. Quite differently, Wolf/Willaert/Pierson in their quantitative study to do with group privacy management on SNS unfortunately take into account only the horizontal level – the sharing and withdrawing of information amongst peers. In this paper, I pursue a critical interest by focusing on vertical relations in regard to group privacy – relations of power-imbalances. Despite their differences in perspective, Wolf/Willaert/Pierson nevertheless provide an important argument for the matter I am concerned with, in that their study shows quite clearly that the indicators for group privacy management do indeed differ from the indicators for individual privacy management. With this finding, they add empirical substance to the claim that it is reductionist to limit group privacy to the sum of a number of individual's interests. Hence, they also conclude by arguing, that more research on group privacy is required.

Three Perspectives on Group Privacy in Times of Big Data

Group Privacy and Mass Tracking

Linnet Taylor, with her investigation of mass tracking *(No place to hide? The ethics and analytics of tracking mobility using mobile phone data)* provides an empirical example of the consequences that might follow from a lack of privacy protection for groups in the digital age. In an exploratory case-study she analyses new forms of tracking mobility using mobile phone data in African countries such as the Ivory Coast. Taylor here very impressively addresses the problems that are being created by a one-sided legibility, which evolves when Western aid organisations use the data of African citizens provided by powerful mobile-phone companies. On top of an increased power asymmetry that results, which is already problematic in itself, Taylor finds further problems evolving from a lack of understanding on both sides: the side of the poorly informed data-subjects who are not aware of what happens with their data and the data-interpreters who often misunderstand the information due to a lack of culturally and socially relevant background knowledge.

By referring to an extreme example, which illustrates cases of mutual misunderstanding paired with extreme power imbalances, Taylor shows how individuals can become subjected to discrimination without even noticing that their personal right to privacy has already been violated. With this, she provides an empirical example showing why privacy harm cannot be answered merely by invoking individual rights. Moreover, Taylor also gives examples of cases, where it is not only the algorithmic creation of groups which is problematic due to a lack of protection-rights, but also the tracking of already existing groups such as a tribe. Here, the individual's privacy might be taken care of through anonymisation, but there might be an ethical violation nevertheless because the misinterpretation or biased interpretation of data about their group can harm group members even when not being identified personally (p. 328). In such cases it is not so much respect for the individual members' privacy which is at stake but respect for the group's privacy as a whole.

Taylor frames the legal and ethical problem we are facing here, by comparing the case with Michel Foucault's critique of catholic confession-practices. In both instances, people are made "legible" in the name of care and protection, but the legibility is one-sided. This is when care turns into control. Often people in Africa use devices produced and programmed in foreign countries, potentially even giving their consent to data storage whilst being unaware of the possible consequences. Since the people being watched are not aware of what is being done with their data, they are not accountable as data subjects and thus not accountable as right holders. Taylor concludes, therefore, that new forms of legibility created through algorithmic tracking make people merely visible to control but yet invisible in terms of agency and rights (p. 331).

Taylor sees one reason for this in an unawareness of group rights when it comes to matters of privacy protection. This lack of awareness justifies keeping it with anonymisation, which refers only to the individual rights dimension of privacy. Another reason that Taylors identifies results from the first one. Since they are only concerned with the rights of the individual, companies which eventually operate the tracking, do not find it necessary to include cultural or sociological background studies on the groups they are aiming at. However, such studies are necessary to avoid misunderstandings and to ensure respect for the cultural properties of the people being made legible.

Case studies such as the one undertaken by Linnet Taylor can very vividly illustrate why thinking of privacy protection only from the perspective of the single individual cannot suffice in the age of big data. However, Taylor unfortunately does not systematise her findings within a more general theoretical framework of group rights, privacy rights, and social theory.

The Collective Dimension of Data Protection

A rather systematic approach including a more comprehensive perspective has been put forward by *Allessandro Mantelero*. In his article titled *"Personal data for decisional purposes in the age of analytics: from an individual to a collective dimension of data protection"* he very convincingly argues why so far all takes on group privacy fall short with regard to what he calls "a collective dimension of data-protection", which he sees violated due to the use of big data. Mantelero's key point thereby concerns the same problematic issues to which Taylor has been alluding. He too sees data-subjects' unawareness as right holders and the power imbalance between the trackers and the tracked as the two major problems related to an individualistic take on group privacy. However, Mantelero is not so much concerned with matters of global injustice between rich and poor countries as he is in decrying injustice resulting from unawareness and power imbalances present today within the European Union. To show this, he refers to a range of empirical studies dealing with new forms of groups generated through algorithms. With relation to different examples (Neighborhood Credit Scores, Target Advertising, Price Discrimination, PredPol), he points out how the newly created forms of groups can be a source of unjust discrimination.

After preparing his argument by means of empirical references, Mantelero provides an extensive overview of existing approaches to group privacy, not only referring to Bloustein but also to other related concepts. He classifies the existing takes into three categories: "group privacy", "organizational privacy", and "extension of individual data protection to collective entities". Although he attributes potentials for integrating a collective dimension to the third category, which conceptualises groups as autonomous entities, Mantelero nevertheless concludes that eventually none of the three takes overcomes an atomistic ontology. However, such ontology solves matters of group rights by reducing them to individual rights (Floridi 2014). Doing so, they cannot solve pressing problems related to unawareness and power-imbalances.

A possible answer for this blind spot in privacy theory can be found in the underlying understanding of what characterises a group as such. Mantelero here differentiates between two dominant sociological strands of group theory. The first is called "individualistic theory" (p. 244) in that it defines the group from the perspective of individual members. It is the theory which underlies the traditional concept of group privacy, within which two criteria are relevant: a) stability/consolidation and b) awareness of membership. Both criteria are inapplicable to new types of groups, having been created through the use of digital technologies. On the one hand, there are new types of groups being formed through social networking on the Internet. Such groups are characterised by their low access threshold and hence enjoy a high dynamic in their membership. On the other hand, new types of groups that are being created by algorithms classifying individuals without their being aware of having been made part of a group. Neither type is in line with individualistic group theory.

Mantelero calls the second sociological strand of group theory "organic theory". Here the group is understood as "an autonomous unit that assumes the form of an organized collective entity". Such an understanding is based on the concept of organizational privacy, which provides a better starting point, therefore, when wanting to react to what Mantelero calls a new dimension of protection: the collective dimension of data-protection. In the central section of his article, Mantelero not only describes this new dimension of protection but also points to its democratic relevance. He convincingly argues that safeguarding the collective dimension of data protection is in line with safeguarding the quality of society, since at stake here are the most fundamental values of democracy. To do so, Manteleo once more refers to the concept of "unjust discrimination", this time more systematically than at the beginning of his article. By referring to the example of price discrimination, he points out how the unjust treatment of different categories of people could be avoided by acknowledging that data protection has a collective dimension which not only refers to individual rights but also to common values. This leads to his drawing parallels between other fields of legal regulation, such as environmental protection. Here the collective representation of common interests (such us equal justice), which cannot be reduced to individual rights, has already found representation in law.

In this regard, Mantelero draws particular attention to the similarities between his claim for a collective concept of data protection and the concept of consumer law. In both fields legal protection refers to the common interest of certain groups of people (users or consumers) but the subjects of the protection have no relationship to each other. However, the difference between both fields is that the potential damages covered by consumer law are often more evident and easier to defend than the damages caused by privacy violation. The latter are usually either of a subtle, ethical nature or difficult to trace back. This difference could hold as an explanation as to why the collective interest in data protection has yet to be recognized, quite unlike consumer or environmental protection.

Finally, Mantelero also thinks about possible solutions on how to exercise a law that reflects the collective interest in data protection. Here he points to the idea of having authorised third parties being responsible for licensing web providers. This idea has already been put forward in terms of individual privacy and personal data protection. Mantelero further suggests extending the risk assessment standards for becoming licensed in regard to the collective dimension of protection. Respective standards should reflect not only the individual interests at stake with privacy but also the collective interests. This requires taking into account ethical and social concerns related to privacy violations. The outcome of a respective extension should be extensive enough, Mantelero concludes, that companies would be encouraged to start working with a broader range of privacy by using design solutions.

With his article on the collective dimension of data protection, Mantelero provides a useful overview of the state of the art regarding group privacy. Not only does he refer to a wide range of empirical studies making visible urgent problems in relation to protection gaps, but he also quite extensively reviews existing privacy concepts dealing with the issue. By doing so, Mantelero also acknowledges the global dimension of data protection in the digital age when turning to both sides of the Atlantic, comparing and relating European and American discourses. Here his focus lies not so much on criticising existing approaches as it does on reviewing them for ideas that might help outlining a common interest-approach to data protection. Even though he identifies a common starting point in the concept of organisational privacy, he nevertheless concludes that so far all existing privacy concepts are suffering from being limited to an individual rights perspective, which cannot suffice to meet the threats posed by big data.

Mantelero locates the roots of their individualistic limitation in their attitude towards groups in general. While there were always people making claims for the irreducibility of a certain quality which can be created by and through social groups (starting with Aristotle's considerations about metaphysics), in the privacy discourse most people reject this idea, maintaining that eventually every group can be reduced to its members. Bloustein, for instance, chose the easy way out of the metaphysical question, simply by taking sides with individualism without further explaining his reasons. However, for Mantelero this cannot be a satisfactory option. He takes a stand contra individualism by stating that "collective data protection concerns collective interests, which are not the mere sum of individual interests" (p. 246). He defines a group, the entity to which such a dimension of data protection applies, as "being characterized by non-aggregative interest" (p. 249).

Indeed, both these statements reject an individualist approach, yet they provide only negations as alternatives (not the mere sum, non-aggregative interests). With this, Mantelero leaves us with more questions than answers. What are collective interests if not aggregative interests? What makes them non-aggregative and how can they be attributed to a group? Without engaging with possible answers to such questions, Mantelero cannot provide a solid argument against common critiques raised by individualists, who claim that collective interests can also be reduced to individual interests. His theoretical approach unfortunately remains underdeveloped in these very central aspects of his claim. The merit, therefore, of what Mantelero himself describes as "an introductory study of a new approach to group privacy" should not so much be searched for in what could be regarded as his own approach as in what is an extremely valuable overview of the most central problems at stake with present day group privacy. Mantelero points us to the most urgent fields of action, one of which is to develop a theoretical basis on which to build a concept of group privacy that is fit to meet the challenges of the digital age.

Group Rights in the Digital Age

Such a basis has been considered by *Albert Ingold*. Even though he is not referring to privacy explicitly, the underlying problem he is concerned with shares common ground with claims for a new approach to group privacy, such as those being put forward by authors like Mantelero, Floridi or Taylor. Ingold is similarly concerned with a lack of protection manifesting in light of new group-phenomenon's being made possible by digital technologies. His theoretical considerations on the matter could be instructive for new approaches to group privacy since he defends an alternative to the individualistic definition of groups. Ingold's major concern in relation to this is to find a model which may also serve to protect such forms of groups legally that are not captured by the traditional definition based on stability and consolidation. His intention is to define a meaning which better reflects a social reality permeated by digitally mediated communication practices.

In his quest for a model which includes legal protection for new forms of groups, Ingold structures his article in a twofold manner. Firstly, he outlines an alternative definition for groups. Secondly, he runs through different scenarios, seeking the best way to fit such an alternative definition of groups into the framework of German law. Ingold starts by describing his concern from an empirical perspective, considering social phenomena such as *smartmobs, flashmobs, facebook-parties* or *hacker-* and *activist-collaborations*. Such collectives are characterised by their dynamic: Their spontaneity, their decentralised structure, by having a low access threshold and thus a high fluctuation of membership. Being featured by such characteristics, they do not fulfill the basic condition of a group as laid down by German law. This condition is to show a certain degree of organisational consolidation.

Even though they do not fulfill the condition, they still deserve to be legally acknowledged as groups and not as mere aggregations of individuals, Ingold claims. To defend his claim, he refers to social theory. He looks at different group theories, especially focusing on those, which move away from taking consolidation as a necessary condition; he instead seeks to define groups from a rather metaphysical perspective. In this way, Ingold manages to pin down the intuition lying behind the negations formulated by Mantelero. Having reviewed a number of standpoints, Ingold concludes that the most adequate theories for this claim are those operating with the concept of "Emergenz" (i.e. Durkheim, Searle, Luhmann). Very roughly, the ontology of *emergence* (direct engl. translation for "Emergenz") could be described as the counterpart to an atomistic ontology. It describes the quality that evolves when the interplay between different elements leads to the creation of new properties. When considered in a social context, one can call such properties emergent if they show a certain kind of coherence. The aggregation of individuals then has developed a quality of its own which is irreducible to its separate parts. This irreducible quality ("Soziale Emergenz") is what differentiates a mere aggregation of individuals from a group.

Most recently the idea of "emergence" has received much attention as it has been made more tangible by a discourse that describes it by invoking the figure of a social swarm. This figure can quite adequately illustrate the special dynamic of technically initiated collective new forms. For instance, it helps to explain why *smartmobs* cannot be reducible to separate contributions. As with a biological swarm, a *smartmob's* smartness is the result of a social dynamic that is being created by a complex nexus of interdependent reactions between individuals, which at some point develops a coherence of its own. The smartness we are dealing with here, therefore, is that of a collectively developed logic rather than that of one person's brain. Along with the new wave of "Emergenz"-theories, by using the social swarm figure to translate an abstract idea into a framework of digital social reality, Ingold proposes to change the definition of groups laid down by German law so that organisational consolidation as a necessary condition would be replaced by *social emergence* ("Sozialer Emergenz").

On the basis of this proposal, Ingold turns in the second part of his article to the German Constitution. He reviews three different models for integrating new definitions into the existing legal framework. Having dismissed the first two models (re-individualisation, objectification) for readily comprehensible reasons, he turns to the only remaining model. This model demands a reconceptualisation of the legal person. This reconfiguration would necessitate a shift from matters of being and existence towards matters of acting. It would imply changing the perspective from collective being towards collective acting when wanting to establish the criterion for when to acknowledge a collective phenomenon as a group that holds certain rights as a legal person. By integrating such a change to the concept of the legal person, it would be possible to leave aside the criterion of organisational consolidation and instead apply social emergence as a necessary but sufficient condition.

Although it generally proposes a very innovative and simultaneously instructive take on how to make group rights fit for the digital age, Ingold's approach unfortunately suffers from a few blind spots. For instance, when wanting to attribute protection rights to digitally generated groups, one has to take into account the fact that most of these groups communicate via social network sites which are provided by commercial entities. Such entities operate by implementing algorithms that follow commercial logics and which influence communication practices. As well as ignoring the fact that many new forms of groups are for the most part being co-created through such algorithms, even with groups which are the result of people consciously using online platforms to network and solidarise, Ingold fails to reflect that algorithms implemented by third parties are still involved (Wambach/Bräunlich 2016). However, this fact needs to be considered when proposing *social emergence* as sufficient condition for a group to hold a right as legal person because the algorithmic involvement might play a central role in the creation of the very coherence that defines the emergence. It thus seems difficult to decide when to speak of socially created emergence ("Soziale Emergenz") and when to speak of technically created emergence when it comes to digitally mediated groups.

Another blind spot concerns the global dimension of digitalisation. When considering possible ways of integrating his new definition of a group into the German legal framework, Ingold ignores the fact that the groups he is concerned with often act globally and are, therefore, hard to attribute to only one legal system. Despite these blind spots, Ingold's idea of legally laying down a new definition of groups based on a concept of *social emergence* nevertheless holds huge inspirational potential, especially in light of the fact that so far we are lacking an appropriate alternative. It seems more than worthwhile, therefore, to think further about *social emergence* as condition for a group to exist as such, and also in regard to group privacy and algorithms.

Discussion

In light of the different arguments reviewed above, it becomes apparent that more research on group privacy is urgently required. All articles call for an approach to group rights that would be elaborated enough to face the challenges lying in store for us with digitalisation. Referring to new group-phenomena made possible through new technologies, they also make strong cases for why their claims are justified. Yet, they all suffer from limitations when it comes to the question of appropriate ways to meet their claims.

Linnet Taylor, in her article on "the ethics and analytics of tracking mobility using mobile phone data" points out serious dangers resulting from an absence of legal regulation when it comes to matters of mass-tracking. Furthermore, she provides possible causes for the dangers involved when criticising the ignorance of powerful agencies regarding cultural and social peculiarities of the people they are tracking. Unfortunately, though, she does not offer any concrete solutions to the problems she has analysed.

Allessandro Mantelero deals with the question of legal regulation regarding algorithmically created groups in his article on "personal data for decisional purposes in the age of analytics: From an individual to a collective dimension of data protection". Here he provides an overview on what is at stake with the collective dimension of data protection. He introduces us to further research on a new approach to group privacy that encompasses the non-aggregative interests implied with group protection in the digital age. To do so, he leaves behind an individual-rights perspective on group privacy, rejecting an individualistic understanding of groups in general. However, in doing so he gives only short shrift to the central but complex question of what could be implied with non-aggregative interests. He also leaves us in the dark when it comes to the question of what an alternative to the individualist understanding of groups would need to imply. His claim for the collective dimension of data-protection generally suffers from a lack of theoretical foundation, without which it is not fit to challenge an atomistic ontology.

Challenging this very ontology can be considered one of the major merits of *Albert Ingold's* article titled "Grundrechtsschutz sozialer Emergenz" (engl. Acknowledging Social Emergence in German Law, own transl.). Ingold here draws on social theory in order to underpin his argument for extending group rights towards metaphysical collective dimensions. By grounding his jurisprudential argument on swarm and emergence theory, Ingold develops a cogent alternative to the individualistic definition of groups, which currently underlies German case law. His aim thereby is to do justice to the potential protection needs of digitally created collectives, which due to their dynamic fail to be covered by present German group law. However, he does not expatiate what dangers he is more explicitly referring to when indicating a lack of legal protection and he also fails to engage with empirically and normatively relevant factors such as the involvement of algorithms and commercial interests. A more specific reflection of the question as to when an extension of group rights would be justified in the name of fundamental values such as justice and freedom could be accomplished by, for instance, linking Ingold's argument with a discourse that deals with the social dimensions of privacy and the values that are at issue (see for instance Rössler/Morkosinska 2015).

Conclusion –
Towards an interdisciplinary account on group privacy

Reviewing three different approaches on the matter of privacy and groups in times of big data, we can find a number of valuable contributions to an issue which calls for urgent consideration. They include an explorative case study, an overview on related legal and empirical discourses together with an approach to group rights, which would enable the inclusion of new group forms within the legal framework. Missing are interdisciplinary links between the different contributions, without which each approach is lacking crucial integrating arguments necessary in developing a group right to privacy that is up to the challenges posed by digitalisation.

Developing such a right calls for interdisciplinary team work, first and foremost because it needs to be thought of as a reaction to empirically proven protection-gaps related to new kinds of groups. Such gaps are to be identified according to fundamental values, found to have been violated due to a lack of regulation. Secondly, empirically proved gaps should lead to a group theory that serves to de-contextualise and hence systematise characteristics and functional chains related to new kinds of collective action in the digital age. Finally, both the empirical findings and related theoretical conceptualisations need to reflect the fundamental values that western democracies consider to be justifying legal regulation. This reflection should ultimately lead to policy recommendations about when and to what extent the privacy of groups operating with and through the use of digital technologies calls for legal protection.

In light of the above, we can see that in order to develop a comprehensive approach to privacy protection for groups which is fit for adoption by policy makers, a new form of interdisciplinary research is needed. Such interdisciplinary research could be considered radical in that it not only involves sharing information and perspectives but also actually requires working together in teams. Such teams need to include at least three disciplinary perspectives: the perspective of empirically specialised disciplines such as empirical anthropology, information or communication science, the perspective of theoretically specialised disciplines such as political, cultural or social theory as well as the normative perspective of legal scholars and ethicists.

Bibliography

Bennet, Colin (2011): "In defence of privacy: The concept and the regime." In: Surveillance & Society 8/4, pp. 485–496.

Bloustein, Edward J. (1978): Individual and Group Privacy, New Brunswick: Transaction Books.

boyd, danah m. (2014): It's complicated. The social lifes of networked teens, New Haven: Yale University Press.

Cohen, Julie E. (2012): Configuring the Networked Self. Law, Code, and the Play of Everyday Practice, New Haven: Yale University Press.

De Wolf, Ralf/Willaert, Koen/Pierson, Jo (2014): "Managing privacy boundaries together: Exploring individual and group privacy management strategies in Facebook." In: Computers in Human Behavior 35, pp. 444–454.

Floridi, Luciano (2014): "Open Data, Data Protection and Group Privacy." In: Philosophical Technology 27, pp. 1–3.

Fuchs, Christian (2011): "Towards an alternative concept of privacy." In: Journal of Information, Communication and Ethics in Society 9/4, pp. 220–237.

Gusy, Christoph/Eichenhover, Johannes/Schulte, Laura (2016): "e-Privacy – von der Digitalisierung der Kommunikation zur Digitalisierung der Privatsphäre." In: Jahrbuch des öffentlichen Rechts der Gegenwart (JöR) 64, pp. 385–409.

Helm, Paula (2016): "Freiheit durch Anonymität? Privatheitsansprüche, Privatheitsnormen und der Kampf um Anerkennung." In: West-End. Neue Zeitschrift für Sozialforschung 1/2016, pp. 133–144.

Ingold, Albert (2014): "Grundrechtsschutz Sozialer Emergenz. Eine Neukonfiguration juristischer Personalität in Art. 19 Abs. 3 GG angesichts webbasierter Kollektivitätsformen." In: Der Staat 53/2, pp. 193–226.

Mantelero, Alessandro (2016): "Personal data for decisional purposes in the age of analytics: from an individual to a collective dimension of data protection." In: Computer Law and Security Review 32/2, pp. 238–255.

Mittelstadt, Brat D./Floridi, Luciano (2015): "The Ethics of Big Data: Current and Foreseeable Issues in Biomedical Contexts." In: Sci Eng Ethics 22/2, pp. 303–41.

Petronio, Sandra (2002): Boundaries of Privacy: Dialectics of Disclosure, Albany, NY: SUNY Press.

Regan, Priscilla M. (2002): "Privacy as a Common Good." In: Information, Communication and Society 5/3, pp. 382–405.

Roberts, Andrew (2014): "A republican account of the value of privacy." In: European Journal of Political Theory 14/3, pp. 320–344.

Rössler, Beate/Mokrosinska, Dorota M. (eds.) (2015): Social Dimensions of Privacy. Interdisciplinary Perspectives, Cambridge: Cambridge University Press.

Rössler, Beate (2015): "Should personal data be a tradable good? On the moral limits of markets in privacy." In: Beate Rössler/Dorota M. Mokrosinska (eds.):

Social Dimensions of Privacy. Interdisciplinary Perspectives, Cambridge: Cambridge University Press, pp. 141–161.

Seubert, Sandra/Becker, Carlos (2016): "Privatheit, kommunikative Freiheit und Demokratie." In: DuD, Datenschutz und Datensicherheit 2/16, pp. 73–78.

Sevignani, Sebastian (2016): Privacy and Capitalism in the Age of Social Media, London: Routledge.

Stahl, Titus (2016): "Indiscriminate mass surveillance and the public sphere." In: Ethics in Information Technology 18, pp. 33–39.

Taylor, Linnet (2015): "No place to hide? The ethics and analytics of tracking mobility using mobile phone data." In: Environment and Planning. Society and Space, doi:10.1177/0263775815608851.

Taylor, Linnet/Floridi, Luciano/van der Sloot, Bart (Eds.): Group privacy: New challenges of data technologies, New York: Springer (forthcoming).

Wambach, Tim/Bräunlich, Katharina (2016): "Retrospective Study of Third-Party Web Tracking." In: Proceedings of the 2nd International Conference on Information Systems Security and Privacy, pp. 138–145.

Warren, Luis/Brandeis, Samuel D. (1890): "The Right to Privacy." In: Harvard Law Rev. 4, p. 193.

Biographical Notes

Mark Coté is a Lecturer in Digital Culture and Society at King's College London.

Paolo Gerbaudo is a Lecturer in Digital Culture and Society at King's College London.

Carolin Gerlitz is Professor for Media Studies – Digital Media and Methods at the University of Siegen and member of the Digital Methods Initiative Amsterdam.

Alexander Gross is an interdisciplinary artist based at the University of Maine.

Paula Helm works as post-doc at Goethe University Frankfurt in the interdisciplinary research-group "Transformations of Privacy".

Marisa McGarry is a Lecturer in Digital Culture at Bowdoin College.

Stefania Milan is Assistant Professor of New Media at the University of Amsterdam and Principal Investigator at DATACTIVE, investigating the evolution of activism vis-à-vis datafication.

Dhiraj Murthy is an Associate Professor at the School of Journalism and the Department of Sociology at the University of Texas at Austin.

Jennifer Pybus is a Senior Lecturer at the London College of Communication.

Ramón Reichert is a Lecturer in Digital Media Culture at the University of Vienna. Since 2014, he has been head of the master's degree Data Studies at Danube University Krems.

Bernhard Rieder is Associate Professor in New Media and Digital Culture at the University of Amsterdam.

Lonneke van der Velden is a Lecturer at the Department of Media Studies of the University of Amsterdam, and a postdoctoral fellow with the DATACTIVE project.